AN INBOX BETWEEN US

David Dean

ISBN 979-8-9944690-0-2 (paperback)

ISBN 979-8-9944690-1-9 (ebook)

Current front cover art/design by David Dean

Original cover design by Aaftab Sheikh

Printed in the United States of America

To my wife and children.

You lived with the weight of my thinking long before it became a book. Thank you for the patience, support, and space you gave me to question, build, and persist.

To the people who stood by me in my work and in my personal life. Those who trusted how I think, what I challenge, and what I try to offer.

Thank you for standing with me, especially when it was not easy or popular.

And to the working world.

You matter.

Your effort, judgment, care, and endurance shape everything we rely on. Thank you for your service, and for being who you are to all of us.

Contents

From the Sender

In the beginning, I hadn't set out to understand organizations. Studying behavior, the patterns and the way we work and how we actually move through a company was never my main objective. That understanding formed over time, the way most true comprehension does, by being close to the work and paying attention to what people actually do when no one is watching.

Early on, I noticed something that didn't quite have a name yet. People didn't follow processes the way they were drawn. They didn't use systems the way they were designed and they didn't make decisions the way leaders assumed they would. Work moved through informal paths, shaped by habit, fear, urgency, personality, and trust. The official version of how work happened rarely matched reality.

At first, that observation sat in the background. It wasn't something I could articulate. It was just a feeling that the story being told about work didn't line up with what I was seeing every day.

Over time, that gap became impossible to ignore.

WHERE THE WORK ACTUALLY HAPPENS

Over the years, I've worked across varying fields of healthcare, enterprise operations, finance, nonprofit environments, HR, IT, frontline support, and cross-functional delivery teams. Some environments were well-funded and polished. Others were fragile and overstretched. What stood out wasn't the maturity of the systems or the sophistication of leadership. It was how consistent human behavior was across all of them.

People improvised when systems didn't fit.

They worked around friction instead of escalating it, made decisions under pressure with incomplete information and they relied on tools they trusted, even when those tools weren't "official."

Ultimately, they built personal and team-level solutions to keep work moving.

In environments where everything appeared controlled from the outside, I still found the same patterns underneath. Shared mailboxes functioning as intake systems. Spreadsheets acting as trackers, queues, or unofficial databases. File shares doubling as document management systems. Email chains carrying decisions that never made it into a system of record.

The scale changed but the behavior didn't.

The more environments I worked in, the clearer it became that organizations don't run on their core systems, rather, they run on whatever people can bend fast enough to meet expectations.

HUMAN RESOURCES: THE BEHAVIORAL CORE

If there was one area that sharpened this lens more than any other, it was Human Resources.

HR sits where policy meets emotion. Every issue that reaches HR already carries weight. Conflict, fear, uncertainty, personal history, organizational power dynamics, legal risk, cultural tension. None of that fits neatly into process diagrams.

Working closely with HR teams meant seeing how often policy had to be interpreted, translated, or stretched to fit reality. It meant watching people navigate situations with no precedent, no clean answer, and no room for error. It meant seeing how much emotional labor sits behind decisions that, from the outside, look procedural.

HR isn't administrative. It's interpretive and behavioral. HR is where the organization reveals how it really treats people under stress.

Building solutions for HR early in my career forced me to understand how people think about fairness, authority, safety, and accountability. It exposed, to me, how different roles experience the same organization in completely different ways. And it made one thing obvious very quickly: most organizational challenges aren't process failures. They're human ones.

IT WAS NEVER ABOUT TECHNOLOGY

Later, as I moved deeper into IT and systems work, that understanding didn't change. It sharpened.

Most "technical issues" weren't technical at all. They were the result of habits, assumptions, misunderstandings, or workarounds that had hardened into routine. When an employee complained that aa process wasn't working, the system was usually doing exactly what it was designed to do. It just wasn't aligned with how the person needed to work.

So I started asking different questions.

What are you trying to accomplish? Why do you do it this way? What happens before this step? What happens when it breaks?

Those questions revealed patterns that were repeated across teams and industries. People gravitated toward tools that let them move quickly and adjust on the fly. Email. Spreadsheets. Shared folders. Notes. Lists. Whatever gave them control.

When core systems couldn't accommodate the nuance of real work, people didn't stop working. They built around them.

What looked like resistance was actually adaptation.

THE INBOX AS THE FRONT DOOR

If there is one place where organizational behavior becomes impossible to hide, it's the inbox.

Email has outlived every productivity trend for a reason. It's flexible. It's forgiving. It doesn't enforce structure unless someone chooses to. And because of that, it absorbs work that has nowhere else to go.

Shared mailboxes, in particular, tell you more about an organization than any dashboard ever could. They show you what work arrives unstructured. They show you what the organization hasn't designed for. They show you where responsibility is unclear, where volume exceeds capacity, where process hasn't caught up with reality.

Most leaders don't see shared mailboxes as systems. The people who use them every day absolutely do.

Across organizations, I saw the same pattern repeat. Business units were told what outcomes were expected of them, given a set of tools, and left to figure out the rest. When formal systems didn't support the work, informal systems filled the gap. Those systems became critical at the team level long before anyone acknowledged them at the organizational level.

When leaders finally saw these workflows up close, the reaction was almost always the same. Confusion. Surprise. The question of why it was being done this way.

The answer was simple. Because it had to be.

PRESSURE MAKES BEHAVIOR VISIBLE

The moments that clarified the most weren't the smooth ones. They were the moments when pressure exposed the fault lines.

Major changes announced without translation. Reorganizations that looked clean on paper and chaotic in practice. Projects where accountability dissolved upward and impact flowed downward. Situations where silence created more damage than bad decisions ever could.

In those moments, it became clear what actually breaks organizations. Not lack of intelligence. Not lack of tools. Not lack of strategy. Avoidance. Ego. Opacity. Fear of ownership.

When leaders don't accept responsibility for the effects of their decisions, the organization compensates in unhealthy ways. Work fragments. Trust erodes. People stop escalating issues and start building workarounds. The gap between intent and execution widens.

The organizations that held together under pressure weren't the ones with the most sophisticated systems. They were the ones where leadership was transparent about impact, honest about tradeoffs, and willing to acknowledge what the work actually required.

STAYING THE SAME PERSON

Living inside that reality shaped how I show up.

Over time, I learned that consistency mattered more than posture. That being the same person in every room reduced friction. That people respond better when they don't have to decode who you're being today.

Whether talking to frontline staff or senior executives, I didn't change my core. The context changed. The expectations changed. The language shifted. But the person didn't.

That consistency made it easier to see patterns without becoming absorbed by them. It made it easier to observe behavior without judging it. And it made it easier to navigate environments where people often felt pressure to perform roles instead of doing the work.

PATTERNS DON'T CARE ABOUT INDUSTRY

After enough exposure, the differences between industries started to matter less than the similarities.

Healthcare. Finance. Enterprise operations. HR. IT. Facilities. Customer service. Different constraints. Different consequences. Same behaviors.

People adapted tools to fit their reality. They built systems where none existed. They relied on what worked, not what was intended. They protected themselves from overload by narrowing focus.

Those patterns didn't change with scale. They just became harder to see.

OBSERVER AND PARTICIPANT

I wasn't watching this from the outside. I was in it. Dealing with the consequences. Cleaning up after decisions. Watching teams absorb the impact of changes they didn't design. Seeing how much invisible work went into keeping things moving.

That dual position mattered. Being close enough to feel the pressure, but far enough away to recognize the pattern. That's where this perspective comes from.

WHY THIS MATTERS NOW

AI isn't entering a clean environment. It's entering this one.

It's stepping into organizations full of informal systems, workarounds, improvised processes, emotional labor, and unspoken rules. It will surface patterns people have learned to live with. It will expose inconsistencies that were previously invisible. It will amplify whatever behavior already exists.

That's why understanding how work really happens matters now. Not as a theory. As a prerequisite.

This book exists to make that reality legible. To help leaders see what their organizations are actually built on. To explain why so many technology initiatives fail without blaming the technology. And to prepare people for what becomes visible when AI joins the system.

Everything that follows builds on this foundation. If you understand the human system you already have, the rest becomes clearer. If you don't, no amount of tooling will save you.

This is the context. This is the message. From the sender.

The Invisible Operating System at Work

Many organizations operate under the assumption that their work is powered by systems. It‘s an easy belief to hold. Systems are tangible. They can be charted, labeled, and assigned owners. They come with governance frameworks, documentation, and performance metrics. They produce artifacts that executives can showcase as proof that operations are orderly and under control.

But what’s visible isn‘t always what’s real.

When leaders talk about “the system,” they‘re usually referring to the official version of how work should proceed, the sanctioned sequence, the approved checkpoints, the tool–driven steps that look neat on a slide deck or inside a workflow application. What they rarely describe is the messy reality of how work actually moves.

In practice, work doesn't glide along the prescribed path. It doesn't arrive at the right entry point, fully formed and ready to go. It doesn't politely wait for missing information or pause until priorities align. Instead, it barges in. It overlaps with other tasks. It competes for attention. It creates urgency long before clarity emerges.

This gap between the documented process and the lived experience isn't a minor discrepancy, it's the heart of the challenge most organizations overlook. Why? Because systems are designed for structure, while real work is shaped by human behavior. Behavior doesn't follow diagrams. It responds to pressure, adapts to ambiguity, and bends rules when necessary. People improvise to keep things moving, even when the official flow says otherwise. The result is a constant negotiation between what the system prescribes and what reality demands.

Until leaders recognize that difference, they'll keep optimizing for an idealized version of work that exists only on paper. The real question isn't "How do we perfect the system?" but "How do we design for the way work truly happens?"

DEFINING THE BEHAVIORAL OPERATING SYSTEM

Every organization operates on two intertwined layers.

The first is the documented operating model, the one leaders design and formalize. It's the visible layer, built from processes, workflows, policies, tools, and reporting structures. It promises order, consistency, and predictability. It is deliberate and explicit, a blueprint for how work should happen.

The second layer is less visible but far more influential: the behavioral operating system. Unlike the first, this one isn't engineered; it emerges. It's made up of the habits, shortcuts, interpretations, coping mechanisms, emotional reactions, and social negotiations that people rely on to get work done when reality refuses to follow the script.

This behavioral layer isn't just "culture" in the abstract. It's the practical infrastructure of human behavior, the set of choices and adjustments that determine how work actually moves forward when the official system collides with uncertainty.

When instructions leave gaps, behavior fills them. When priorities clash, behavior decides what wins. When risk feels ambiguous, behavior sets the pace. And when accountability feels unsafe, behavior shifts toward self-preservation.

This layer never sleeps. Even when the documented system functions perfectly, people are still making judgment calls, how closely to follow the rules, when to bend them, and when to bypass them entirely.

The mistake most organizations make is treating this behavioral layer as noise, as deviation from the "real" system. In truth, it's the opposite. Behavior is the operating model. The documented system is simply an attempt to shape it.

So the question isn't whether behavior matters, it's whether leaders are willing to design with it in mind.

WHY THE INBOX MATTERS AND WHY IT MUST BE BOUNDED

If behavior truly functions as the organization's operating system, the next question is: where can we see it most clearly? The answer isn't "everywhere," and it certainly isn't buried in vague notions of culture. Those ideas are too broad to offer practical insight. What we need is a surface where behavior shows up consistently, under pressure, and in real time.

That surface is the inbox.

Not because email is elegant or efficient. Not because it's the best-designed tool. The inbox matters for a simpler reason: it leaves evidence. It captures the fingerprints of behavior as work unfolds.

This distinction is critical. The inbox is not the system itself. It doesn't represent the entirety of work or the whole organization. Treating it that way would be a mistake. Instead, think of it as a diagnostic lens, a place where interpretation becomes visible.

Look closely, and patterns emerge. Delay signals hesitation. Forwarding reflects uncertainty. Overly detailed justifications hint at fear. Crisp, direct responses reveal confidence. The inbox doesn't create these behaviors; it records them.

That makes it uniquely valuable. Unlike formal systems, which demand compliance before expression, the inbox allows raw behavior to surface. People don't need perfect clarity to send a message. They don't need alignment to escalate an issue. They don't need certainty to copy someone in. Communication happens before the polish, before the rationalization, before the abstraction.

And that is why the inbox tells the truth about how work really functions. It captures the messy, unfiltered decisions that formal diagrams can never show. If you want to understand the real operating system, the behavioral one, start by studying the traces it leaves behind.

THE INBOX: THE REAL WORKSPACE

For most employees, the inbox is where work feels tangible. Not because every task lives there, but because this is the space where signals arrive and decisions begin. Before work is executed in systems or meetings, it is interpreted, prioritized, negotiated, and often emotionally processed inside the inbox.

People start and end their day there not out of inefficiency, but because the inbox acts as the nerve center of organizational life. It's where urgency announces itself. It's where expectations whisper rather than shout. It's where responsibility stops being abstract and becomes personal.

A task in a project tool is theoretical until it lands in someone's inbox. A deadline becomes urgent when it carries a name. A risk feels real when a manager is copied. In this way, the inbox shapes how employees experience their role, what seems critical, what feels risky, what appears ambiguous, and what feels safe to ignore.

This isn't a breakdown in discipline; it's how human cognition works. Work is rarely experienced as a neat sequence of steps. It arrives as a stream of interruptions, choices, and trade-offs. The inbox mirrors that reality better than any formal system ever has.

That's why it endures, even as new tools emerge. Chat platforms make quick exchanges easier. Workflow systems formalize approvals. Project dashboards organize plans. Yet none of these replace the inbox, because none of them absorb ambiguity without friction.

The inbox doesn't demand perfect clarity. It doesn't insist on completeness or enforce strict order. It offers flexibility in the face of complexity, a way to manage uncertainty without resolving it entirely. In a world where work is fluid and unpredictable, that adaptability is why the inbox remains indispensable.

WHY SYSTEMS CANNOT COMPETE WITH THE INBOX

Formal systems exist to impose order, and that is both their advantage and their Achilles' heel. They operate on assumptions: that inputs will be stable, roles clearly defined, and decision points unambiguous. But human work rarely fits that mold.

When information is incomplete, systems hesitate. When context disappears, they falter. When accountability blurs, they escalate or collapse. In those moments, the inbox quietly steps in, absorbing the friction and keeping work moving.

That's why employees turn the inbox into a Swiss Army knife, a task list, a knowledge archive, an escalation channel, a memory trigger, and a safety net. Not because it's elegant, but because it tolerates the disorder that formal systems are designed to reject.

For leaders, this creates a dangerous blind spot. Systems display the idealized version of work, the clean, structured flow that looks good on dashboards. The inbox reveals the improvisation required to make progress when reality refuses to cooperate.

By the time information reaches leadership through official channels, it has been filtered, summarized, and stripped of emotional weight. What executives see is a polished narrative, not the raw struggle. And here's the kicker: the inbox of a senior leader bears little resemblance to the inbox of someone on the front lines. That gap isn't cosmetic, it explains much of the misalignment organizations wrestle with every day.

DOCUMENTED WORK VERSUS LIVED WORK

When leaders emphasize process adherence, they're usually referring to the documented layer, the official blueprint of how work should flow. Employees, on the other hand, speak from the lived layer, the reality of getting things done amid shifting priorities and incomplete information.

These two narratives coexist, but they tell very different stories. The documented version promises order and coherence. The lived version feels fragmented: tasks appear without warning, priorities change without explanation, dependencies surface late, and expectations are often implied rather than stated. Accountability, meanwhile, feels uneven and unpredictable.

In this environment, the inbox becomes the negotiation table where contradictions are resolved in real time. It's where people decide what matters now, what can wait, when to ask for help, and who to include to stay safe. These choices rarely appear in any system, yet they shape outcomes more reliably than formal process steps ever could.

Studying the inbox isn't about monitoring or micromanaging, it's about uncovering the behavioral logic that drives execution when structure meets uncertainty. If leaders want predictability, they must understand the layer where unpredictability is absorbed and transformed into action.

That layer isn't the documented process. It's the human behavior surrounding it, the improvisation, judgment, and adaptation that keep work moving when the map no longer matches the terrain.

DRIFT IS NOT FAILURE

When leaders compare the official operating model to what they see happening on the ground, the gap is often labeled as failure: the process wasn't followed, the handoff collapsed, the timeline slipped, someone bypassed the system. It's a tidy explanation, but a misleading one.

What looks like failure is usually drift. And drift isn't rebellion; it's adaptation. It's the human response to pressure when reality refuses to fit the assumptions baked into the system. Drift begins where documentation runs out.

No process anticipates every edge case. No workflow predicts every ambiguity. No role description covers every moment of uncertainty. When those gaps appear, people don't freeze, they improvise. They reinterpret instructions, patch missing logic, borrow context from experience, and lean on trust when formal authority feels too rigid.

This isn't chaos. It's patterned behavior. Those patterns decide whether work stays coherent or slowly unravels. They are the invisible architecture of execution, the behavioral operating system that keeps progress alive when the formal one falters.

And if you want to see those patterns, look at the inbox. It's the surface where adaptation leaves its fingerprints: the forwarding that signals uncertainty, the copied names that signal risk, the tone that signals confidence or fear. The inbox doesn't cause drift, it reveals it. For leaders, that makes it less a communication tool and more a diagnostic lens into how work truly happens.

THE MOMENT THAT ACTUALLY MATTERS

If you want to see how work truly moves, focus on a single, fleeting moment, not when a task is logged in a system, not when a form is submitted, not when a status flips. The moment that matters is when someone opens a message.

That instant is brief, but it's packed with judgment. Before any documented step occurs, the reader silently makes choices that will shape everything that follows. These choices rarely feel like decisions; they seem instinctive. But they're not. They're deliberate, compressed into seconds.

In that pause, a mental checklist fires:

Should I act now or later?

Is this urgent or just noisy?

Do I even understand what's being asked?

Am I the right person, or should I redirect?

What happens if I get this wrong?

Do I need to protect myself?

These aren't abstract questions. They're practical filters, shaping behavior before the system ever enters the picture. The inbox is where this pre-system layer of work lives, a space where interpretation precedes execution, where priorities and risks are weighed in real time.

If you study the inbox, you're not just looking at messages. You're observing the hidden architecture of decision-making, the quiet negotiations that determine whether work accelerates, stalls, or shifts direction long before any workflow tool records a single step.

MICRO-DECISIONS AND THEIR CONSEQUENCES

Most organizations overlook how much work happens before a task ever appears in a system. By the time someone clicks "submit" or moves an item forward, they've already navigated a series of micro-decisions, each one shaping the eventual outcome.

In those early moments, the questions come fast: Should I read this carefully or just skim? Respond now or wait until I feel certain? Ask for clarification or try to figure it out alone? Forward it to someone who's seen this before? Include my manager to stay safe? Adjust my tone to avoid conflict?

None of these choices are captured by dashboards, yet they influence speed, accuracy, quality, and even trust. A delay that looks like inefficiency may actually signal hesitation. An escalation might reflect fear rather than complexity. A completed task could represent compliance without true understanding.

This invisible layer of decision-making is where work really begins. And the inbox is the only place that preserves these signals. It records behavior at the moment it forms, before it's polished, normalized, or abstracted away by formal systems. If leaders want to understand why work moves the way it does, they need to look beyond the workflow and into the inbox, where the real story starts.

WHY LEADERS RARELY SEE THIS LAYER

Most leaders rarely encounter the raw reality of work because their position insulates them from it. As people climb the organizational ladder, their inbox evolves. It becomes cleaner, more polished, and heavily curated. Instead of fragments, they see summaries. Instead of uncertainty, they see escalations. Instead of deliberation, they see decisions.

This shift isn't the result of secrecy, it's the result of behavioral adaptation. Messages change as they move upward. Employees communicate differently when authority is involved. They compress complexity, strip away emotional signals, and turn confusion into questions that sound composed. Ambiguity is resolved before it reaches leadership, often through improvisation and quiet negotiation.

By the time an issue lands in an executive inbox, the behavioral work is already complete. The hesitation, the fear, the back-and-forth, the protective maneuvers, all gone. What remains is a sanitized version of reality.

And that creates a powerful illusion. Leaders believe they are observing the system in action, when in truth they are seeing the residue of human effort, the adaptations that filled the gaps the system couldn't cover. The map looks neat because the terrain was smoothed before they saw it.

THE INBOX AS AN EMOTIONAL RECORD

Every inbox doubles as an emotional ledger. Not in a dramatic sense, but in a practical one, tone, timing, length, and even silence carry signals. They reveal how people feel about the work in front of them and the conditions surrounding it.

Patterns emerge when you look closely. One person fires back quickly, but with a defensive edge. Another writes paragraphs to justify a simple action. Someone else waits, holding off until the risk feels lower. Others escalate early, not because the issue is complex, but because blame feels dangerous.

These aren't quirks of personality; they're adaptive behaviors shaped by perceived risk, clarity, and trust. Psychological safety changes how a message sounds. Certainty about expectations changes how fast someone responds. When those anchors are missing, communication becomes a form of self-protection.

The inbox makes these dynamics visible. It's where people manage the emotional cost of work, where confidence shows up as brevity, and fear hides behind formality. If you want to understand the human side of execution, start by reading between the lines.

SILENCE IS NOT ABSENCE

Silence is one of the most misunderstood signals in organizational life. In formal systems, it often masquerades as success, no alerts, no escalations, no logged issues. Everything looks stable. But in the inbox, silence tells a different story.

It can signal uncertainty, avoidance, fear of making a mistake, or sheer overload. When someone doesn't respond, they're not passive; they're making a choice. Maybe they're waiting for clarity. Maybe they're weighing how to phrase a reply without triggering conflict. Maybe they're protecting themselves from risk.

This hesitation leaves traces, delayed responses, half-written drafts, indirect language, but those traces never appear in dashboards. Systems register absence as compliance. The inbox reveals it as tension.

Leaders who interpret silence as agreement risk missing one of the most important behavioral cues available to them. Silence isn't neutral; it's active. It speaks volumes about trust, psychological safety, and the hidden cost of decision-making. The question isn't whether silence means something, it's whether leaders are willing to listen to what it's saying.

BEHAVIORAL DIVERSITY INSIDE THE SAME ORGANIZATION

One reason the inbox serves as such a powerful diagnostic lens is that it exposes the uneven way people experience the same piece of work. Organizations often speak about consistency as if it were achievable, but consistency depends on shared interpretation, and shared interpretation is rare.

The same message does not land uniformly. A finance professional scans for accuracy and justification. An operations leader zeroes in on urgency and downstream impact. An HR partner reads through the prism of risk and policy. A technologist looks for feasibility and constraints. Each perspective acts like a behavioral filter, shaping what happens next.

These filters explain why work rarely moves in straight lines. It's not inefficiency, it's divergence. People are navigating different mental models, different priorities, and different definitions of risk while trying to coordinate action. The inbox captures this complexity because it records responses in real time, before they are smoothed out by formal systems.

If you study the inbox, you see the branching paths of interpretation, the subtle decisions that turn a single signal into multiple trajectories. That's the hidden architecture of execution: not a failure of discipline, but the reality of human cognition under pressure.

THREADS AS BEHAVIORAL MAPS

Long email threads that span roles and teams offer a rare window into how the real operating model takes shape. Follow one from start to finish and you can watch the dynamics unfold like a slow-motion negotiation.

It often begins with a message that feels tentative, a loosely framed request or an ambiguous question. Early replies try to impose clarity or define boundaries. Then, as more participants join, the tone shifts. Authority gets negotiated. Interpretations collide. Misunderstandings surface like cracks in the pavement.

Eventually, the thread reaches a tipping point. Sometimes it stabilizes, appearing to signal alignment, though that alignment may mask quiet resignation or a workaround everyone agrees to tolerate. Other times, the thread fractures. Collapse can look like escalation to higher authority, prolonged silence, or the emergence of parallel conversations that never reconnect.

This progression isn't random. It mirrors how people interpret power, risk, and responsibility inside the organization. And while meetings erase this arc and systems flatten it into clean status updates, the inbox preserves it in full detail, a behavioral storyline hiding in plain sight.

WHERE REAL EXPERTISE ACTUALLY LIVES

Inbox behavior often exposes where true expertise lives inside an organization. When uncertainty strikes, people rarely turn to documentation first, they turn to other people. And not just anyone, but those who have proven helpful before.

These individuals become quiet stabilizers. Their inboxes tell the story: forwarded threads seeking interpretation, discreet questions that never make it into a formal system, requests for guidance delivered with trust. Their influence isn't tied to title or hierarchy; it stems from something rarer, the ability to provide clarity without judgment.

Organizations frequently underestimate how much progress depends on these informal anchors. Dashboards won't reveal it.

Workflow tools won't capture it. But the inbox does. By studying patterns of reliance rather than formal ownership, leaders can uncover where the organization truly balances itself, and where resilience quietly resides.

EMOTIONAL RELIABILITY AND WORK DISTRIBUTION

Over time, work tends to orbit around those who offer emotional steadiness. These are the colleagues others trust to respond without panic, to think clearly under pressure, and to guide decisions without adding risk. They may not hold the deepest technical expertise, yet they often become the most relied upon.

Their inboxes reveal this gravitational pull. Questions cluster there. Requests for clarification and validation accumulate quietly, forming an invisible layer of labor that rarely shows up in workload metrics or performance reviews.

The inbox makes this imbalance visible. It shows where emotional weight gathers, and where resilience silently carries the organization forward.

WHY THIS LAYER CANNOT BE IGNORED

None of this behavior happens by chance. It emerges because people are working inside systems that cannot fully anticipate human complexity. When leaders overlook this layer, they often misread what they see. A delay looks like inefficiency. A workaround looks like resistance. A deviation looks like a training gap. In truth, these patterns are usually rational adaptations, people adjusting to keep progress alive when the formal design falls short.

The inbox doesn't just confirm that adaptation exists; it explains why. It captures the friction points, the moments where judgment replaces procedure, and the choices that keep work moving despite ambiguity.

Understanding this reality doesn't require surveillance or prying into private messages. It requires a shift in perspective, seeing the inbox not as a communication tool, but as evidence of a deeper operating model at work. That model is behavioral, and it is always present.

The real question isn't whether this layer exists. It does. The question is whether leaders are prepared to acknowledge it, and design with it in mind.

CULTURE AS AN OUTCOME, NOT A VARIABLE

Organizations often speak about culture as if it floats above the work, something soft, atmospheric, shaped by mission statements, leadership messages, or the occasional survey. But culture isn't a parallel system. It's an outcome. It forms when behavior repeats under similar conditions long enough to become predictable.

And the inbox is where that repetition leaves its clearest trace.

Every forwarded message, every copied manager, every delayed reply tells a story. A cautious tone here, an over-explained justification there, these aren't isolated acts. They are signals of what the organization rewards, tolerates, or punishes. Over time, those signals harden into norms, and norms become culture.

This is why the inbox matters. It doesn't record aspirational values or polished statements; it captures what people actually do when the stakes feel real. It shows the choices made under pressure, the instinct to protect, the hesitation to act, the need to justify. These micro-decisions accumulate quietly, shaping the lived experience of work far more than any formal declaration.

If leaders want to understand their culture, they shouldn't start with what's written on the walls. They should start with what's written in the inbox, because that's where the truth of behavior becomes visible.

WHY PROCESSES FAIL QUIETLY

Processes rarely collapse overnight, they wear down slowly. Erosion begins the moment the documented steps stop matching the reality people face. That gap creates friction. Friction invites workarounds. Workarounds, repeated often enough, harden into habits. Eventually, the process still exists on paper, but the real work has migrated elsewhere.

And the inbox is where that migration leaves its trail.

When instructions lack clarity, people turn to email for interpretation. When ownership feels murky, responsibility gets negotiated in threads. When formal approvals drag, informal signoff arrives through copied names. None of this appears as failure in a dashboard. The system still shows completed steps and reasonable timestamps. But the substance of execution has shifted into an informal layer the system doesn't acknowledge.

By the time leaders notice outcomes wobbling, the behavioral divergence is already entrenched. Postmortems then circle the surface: the process wasn't followed, training fell short, the system needs enhancement. These explanations miss the deeper truth, that adaptation began long before the breakdown became visible.

The inbox would have shown the cracks forming. It preserves the early signals: hesitation, improvisation, negotiation. If leaders want to prevent erosion, they need to study where work actually moves when structure starts to fail, not after the collapse, but while the drift is still reversible.

THE DIFFERENCE BETWEEN COMPLIANCE AND ALIGNMENT

One of the most persistent illusions in organizational life is the assumption that compliance equals alignment. Systems excel at enforcing compliance, they make sure fields are filled, steps are checked off, and statuses are updated. But none of that guarantees understanding, conviction, or trust in the process. A completed workflow can mask deep uncertainty.

The inbox exposes this gap. When behavior is aligned, communication feels confident: messages are clear and concise, clarifying questions diminish over time, and escalations happen for legitimate reasons rather than as a defensive reflex. When behavior is merely compliant, the tone shifts. Responses grow long and cautious. Language hedges. Requests for confirmation multiply. Extra names appear on CC lines as a shield. Decisions stall until responsibility feels diluted.

Both patterns satisfy the system. Both look identical on a dashboard. Yet only one produces outcomes that are reliable and resilient. The other creates fragility disguised as order.

Leaders who rely exclusively on system-level signals see completion, not conviction. The real story, the difference between alignment and mere compliance, lives in the inbox, where behavior speaks louder than checkmarks.

PSYCHOLOGICAL SAFETY AND MESSAGE SHAPE

Psychological safety is often treated as an abstract concept, but the inbox makes it tangible. Every message carries signals about how safe someone feels. When confidence is high, communication tends to be clear and direct. When safety erodes, the tone changes, messages grow layered, explanations multiply, and language softens to avoid friction. Extra recipients appear on CC lines, not for collaboration, but as a shield against risk.

These patterns aren't deliberate strategies; they're instinctive responses to uncertainty. And they accumulate quietly, long before engagement scores reveal trouble. In organizations where psychological safety is low, the inbox tells the story: threads stretch longer, decisions slow down, and escalations happen sooner than they should.

The signals aren't hard to read once you know what to look for. They show that safety isn't a slogan, it's a lived condition, and the inbox is where its absence leaves the clearest trace.

WHY SURVEYS MISS WHAT THE INBOX SHOWS

Employee surveys ask people to compress months of experience into a handful of abstract questions. By the time responses are given, memory has blurred details, social desirability has softened honesty, and fatigue has shaped tone. These tools capture reflection, not reality.

The inbox, by contrast, records experience as it unfolds. Stress shows up in delayed replies, not weeks later. Confusion appears in fragmented threads, not as a neat summary. Trust reveals itself through behavior, who gets copied, who gets asked, not through checkbox agreement.

Surveys aren't useless, but they are incomplete. Leaders who rely only on retrospective tools will always be reacting to the past instead of anticipating what's coming.

WHEN LEADERSHIP BECOMES BLIND

Leadership blindness rarely stems from intent; it grows out of structure. As people advance through the organization, the texture of the information they receive changes. Their inbox shifts from being a space of ambiguity to one of resolution. What they see are polished decisions, not the messy deliberations that preceded them.

This creates an illusion of coherence. Alignment appears real because the signals reaching leadership look aligned. Yet that neatness often hides the long behavioral negotiations that happened out of sight, negotiations shaped by fear, adaptation, and compromise.

By the time an issue reaches the executive level, it has already been filtered and softened. The raw uncertainty, the hesitation, the improvisation, all gone. If leaders want to understand the true state of work, they need to look closer to the edge of execution, where inboxes still tell the unvarnished story.

ORGANIZATIONAL HEALTH LIVES IN PATTERNS

Healthy organizations aren't defined by the absence of challenges, they're defined by how people behave when challenges appear. The inbox makes this visible in ways dashboards never do.

In environments where trust and clarity exist, messages tend to be crisp and purposeful. Questions replace defensive explanations. Threads resolve quickly instead of spiraling into endless negotiation. Escalations happen when they should, signaling urgency rather than fear.

Contrast that with unhealthy patterns: long chains filled with justification, silence where clarity should live, and escalations used as shields instead of solutions. These aren't random quirks; they're the accumulated result of incentives, leadership signals, and the consequences people have learned to expect.

The inbox becomes the archive of these behaviors, a living record of how an organization metabolizes uncertainty. If you want to know whether your culture is resilient, start by studying the patterns hiding in plain sight.

WHY LEADERS MISATTRIBUTE ROOT CAUSES

When processes falter or results drift, leaders often default to familiar levers: update the documentation, schedule more training, roll out another system. These steps can help, but they rarely solve the deeper issue. Structure alone doesn't change outcomes, behavior does.

The inbox offers an early signal of whether that shift is happening. It reveals trust in the process, clarity of expectations, and the confidence to act without fear. Metrics will confirm success later, but the inbox whispers it first. Ignore that layer, and surprises aren't just possible, they're inevitable.

THE INBOX AS CULTURAL EVIDENCE

Everything leaders hope to measure about culture is already visible in inbox behavior. Speed and clarity signal trust. Delay and diffusion hint at fear. Brevity often reflects alignment, while repetition exposes confusion. Culture isn't declared in meetings, it's enacted in the quiet moments when choices feel personal. If you want the truth, it's written in the inbox, not on the walls.

WHY THIS MATTERS BEFORE AI ENTERS THE PICTURE

Before any new technology, especially AI, is introduced, leaders need a clear picture of the behavioral terrain it will operate in. AI can process steps, but it cannot read hesitation or interpret fear. It doesn't understand why someone copies a manager instead of replying directly. If implementation is based solely on documented workflows, the foundation is incomplete because those workflows omit the human logic that drives real decisions.

The inbox exposes that missing layer. It shows the nuance systems overlook, the adaptations, the caution, the trust gaps. Without this understanding, organizations risk automating assumptions rather than improving outcomes.

WHY AI EXPOSES WHAT ORGANIZATIONS PREFER NOT TO SEE

When organizations bring AI into their operations, the conversation often centers on efficiency, automating tasks, accelerating workflows, reducing human variability. It sounds logical, but it overlooks what AI actually encounters once deployed.

AI doesn't step into a pristine system. It enters a living ecosystem of behavior. It meets work shaped by interpretation rather than rigid instruction, decisions made under pressure rather than certainty, and informal norms that quietly override formal rules. Much of the real work happens before a system records a step, or entirely outside the system AI is designed to optimize.

The inbox is where this reality leaves its clearest trace. It shows the negotiations, the hesitations, the improvisations that define execution. When leaders implement AI without studying these patterns, they end up training technology on an imagined organization, the one described in documentation, while the human organization continues to operate on its behavioral operating system.

This disconnect isn't a technical flaw; it's a modeling failure. AI learns the map, not the terrain. And when the terrain is full of ambiguity, adaptation, and emotional logic, efficiency initiatives risk reinforcing assumptions instead of improving outcomes. Before automation begins, leaders must ask: Are we teaching AI how work is supposed to happen, or how it actually does?

AUTOMATION WITHOUT BEHAVIORAL CONTEXT

AI systems excel at spotting patterns, but patterns only matter when they're understood in context. A delayed response might look like hesitation, but without insight into the risk environment, that interpretation is guesswork. Escalations can signal complexity, or fear. High message volume might mean overload, or it might mean avoidance. Strip away behavioral context, and AI ends up amplifying surface signals while missing the forces that shape them.

This is why so many AI-driven transformations start strong and fade fast. They deliver speed without substance, optimizing throughput while ignoring meaning, accelerating workflows without addressing interpretation, formalizing steps while informal behavior quietly persists. The result is a system that looks efficient but fails to change how work actually happens.

The inbox exposes this disconnect early. It captures the nuance AI overlooks, the hesitation before action, the defensive escalation, the subtle markers of trust or uncertainty. If leaders want AI to transform more than metrics, they must teach it to see beyond the documented process and into the behavioral logic that drives execution. Otherwise, automation becomes a mirror of assumptions rather than a lever for progress.

WHY TRANSFORMATION EFFORTS STALL

Many transformation efforts fail, and the postmortem explanation often sounds familiar: people resisted. They didn't adopt the tool. They ignored the process. They slipped back into old habits. These narratives make resistance sound like a personal flaw, when in reality, it's structural.

Behavior doesn't revert out of stubbornness, it adapts to survive. When a new system adds cognitive strain, amplifies ambiguity, or heightens personal risk, people compensate. They do what feels safest in the environment they inhabit.

The inbox makes this compensation visible. You see messages seeking reassurance before action, threads that create parallel channels outside the official workflow, and language that documents defensively rather than decisively. These aren't signs of poor attitude; they're signals of misalignment between the formal system and the behavioral operating system underneath it.

Transformation stalls when leaders misread these signals as obstacles instead of insights. Every hesitation, every workaround, every cautious escalation is data about the friction the system introduced. Ignoring that data guarantees failure. The question isn't "Why won't people change?", it's "What conditions make the old behavior feel safer than the new one?" Until leaders answer that, technology will keep advancing while adoption lags behind.

BEHAVIORAL LITERACY AS A LEADERSHIP SKILL

Understanding inbox behavior isn't about tracking messages or scrutinizing individuals, it's about learning to interpret the signals an organization sends. This skill, often called behavioral literacy, means recognizing what lies beneath the surface: when hesitation reflects fear rather than laziness, when delays stem from uncertainty instead of resistance, and when agreement masks mere compliance rather than true alignment.

Leaders who develop this literacy approach conversations differently. They wonder why a decision took so long to emerge, why a discussion keeps spiraling instead of reaching closure, or why authority figures are copied on emails instead of expectations being clarified. These questions don't lead to new software or faster workflows; they lead to insight.

The inbox, in this sense, becomes more than a communication tool, it's a diagnostic instrument. Every thread, every CC, every delay offers clues about how people think, feel, and respond. Reading those clues well is what turns information into understanding.

PREDICTABILITY COMES FROM INTERPRETATION, NOT CONTROL

Organizations often chase predictability by tightening control, adding rules, layering steps, and enforcing compliance. That strategy only works when people already act in ways that match the intent behind those rules. When they don't, control doesn't create stability; it creates friction.

True consistency comes from shared interpretation. People need to see work through a similar lens, understand expectations, weigh risks, and trust one another. Without that alignment, predictability is an illusion.

The inbox reveals whether this alignment exists. A short thread often signals clarity. A well-framed question suggests psychological safety. A direct escalation reflects confidence in leadership. These aren't abstract indicators; they're operational realities, visible in everyday communication.

THE INBOX AS EARLY WARNING SYSTEM

One of the most valuable aspects of inbox awareness is its ability to reveal trouble before the numbers do. Long before metrics dip or KPIs start to slide, behavior begins to shift. Conversations stretch out, replies take longer, and escalation becomes more frequent. These subtle changes show up in inbox patterns well ahead of formal reports. Leaders who can interpret these signals gain something rare: time. Time to make structural adjustments instead of scrambling reactively. Time to recalibrate expectations before trust begins to fracture.

WHY THIS CHAPTER COMES FIRST

This chapter isn't about promoting email as the ultimate tool, it's about elevating behavioral visibility into a leadership discipline. The inbox appears first because it offers the simplest entry point for observing how work truly happens. No new platform, no extra dashboards, no elaborate frameworks, just a shift in what leaders pay attention to.

When that shift occurs, the fog lifts. Culture becomes something you can see rather than speculate about. Processes reveal themselves instead of being assumed. Even AI feels less like magic and more like mechanics. In short, behavior turns from invisible patterns into legible signals leaders can act on.

SEEING THE ORGANIZATION AS IT IS

The inbox isn't a flaw to fix; it's a lens into how an organization truly operates. Every message reflects something deeper, how people respond under pressure, how responsibility shifts, how uncertainty is managed. These patterns form an invisible operating system that already drives the business, whether leaders acknowledge it or not.

Ignoring this layer doesn't make it disappear; it only guarantees surprise when cracks appear. Understanding it doesn't demand flawless execution, it calls for curiosity, humility, and the courage to admit that the real operating model is far more human than the one sketched on a whiteboard. Leaders who learn to read these signals stop guessing and start seeing.

THE FOUNDATION FOR WHAT COMES NEXT

Everything in this book rests on a single premise: transformation begins with understanding behavior. When leaders overlook how human patterns shape work, systems inevitably disappoint. When they ignore the role of interpretation, culture remains a slogan rather than a lived reality. And when they assume technology will compensate for misunderstanding, it magnifies confusion instead of creating clarity.

The inbox is not the entire story, but it leaves the clearest trace of how the story unfolds. Every thread, every escalation, every silence offers evidence of the operating system beneath the diagrams, the one that actually runs the organization. Seeing that layer requires more than process maps; it requires attention. Leaders who learn to read these signals stop chasing illusions and start engaging with reality. That is the first step toward change that lasts.

Human Patterns Behind Process Bottlenecks

PRESSURE IS THE FIRST INPUT

Many organizations assume their processes are solid because they mistake design for reality. A diagram, a flowchart, or a neat set of swim lanes creates an illusion of stability. The logic seems obvious: if the instructions are clear, people will follow them.

That assumption collapses the moment real-world pressure enters the picture. Processes rarely fail because the documentation was flawed; they fail because stress reshapes behavior before anyone even reaches the first decision point.

Pressure is not abstract, it arrives in tangible forms: overwhelming volume, urgent deadlines, ambiguous priorities, compressed timelines, accountability without authority, and emotional stakes that weigh heavily on individuals. It manifests as too many requests at once, conflicting expectations, or tasks that carry personal or ethical significance. And it never distributes evenly. It pools in certain roles, at critical handoffs, and at moments where the margin for error disappears.

Leaders often miss this dynamic. They encounter pressure as numbers on a dashboard or as escalations in a meeting. Meanwhile, the frontline feels it viscerally, through fatigue, tension, and the constant need to keep work moving despite the squeeze.

A process that looks elegant in calm conditions behaves unpredictably when pressure becomes the norm. This isn't about discipline or intent; it's about how stress rewires cognition. Under strain, attention narrows, decisions accelerate, tradeoffs multiply, and survival instincts override optimization.

By the time a workaround appears or a deviation occurs, the environment has already shifted. Pressure doesn't wait for a failure point, it sets the stage for every choice that follows.

This is the starting point for true clarity: pressure isn't a secondary factor. It is the first input into every workflow, shaping outcomes long before the process map ever comes into play.

PRESSURE COLLIDES WITH HUMAN LIMITS

Human capacity has limits. Attention, memory, emotional balance, and decision-making strength all erode when pressure persists, not because people are broken, but because biology sets boundaries.

Any process that assumes constant focus, flawless recall, emotional detachment, and infinite cognitive bandwidth is built on an illusion. As pressure rises, the gap between what the process expects and what humans can deliver grows wider.

People under strain don't stop caring; they stop operating in the way the designer imagined. Priorities shift. Urgency takes precedence over sequence. Visibility and personal risk overshadow optimization. Systematic execution gives way to situational judgment.

And then the silent questions begin:

What happens if I get this wrong?

Will slowing down make things worse?

Who will notice? Who will feel the impact if I escalate?

What will this decision say about me?

These questions never appear in a workflow diagram, yet they dominate under pressure. They become the real decision framework.

This is where structural failure begins, not at a broken step, but at the assumption that execution is rational and evenly distributed. In reality, pressure introduces asymmetry and emotional consequence.

From that moment forward, behavior changes. The process map remains the same, but the operating environment has shifted.

COMPENSATION BEGINS QUIETLY

When pressure rises beyond what a process anticipates, people adapt. These adaptations aren't acts of defiance, they're survival strategies meant to keep work moving when the official route becomes too expensive in time, effort, or risk.

Adaptation takes many shapes. Sometimes it means accelerating steps. Sometimes skipping a check. Other times, adding an informal safeguard or quietly solving a problem instead of escalating it. It might even mean honoring the intent of a rule while bending its letter.

What matters most is that these adjustments are hyper-local. They happen in the moment, at the level of the individual, responding to conditions no process map could fully predict. They're rarely coordinated, almost never documented.

At this stage, the process hasn't collapsed. The human system is compensating for its blind spots.

This is where leaders often misread the situation. They see deviation and assume noncompliance. In reality, they're witnessing a form of load balancing, a person redistributing cognitive and emotional weight to keep the system afloat.

Why does this happen? Because the process asks for more than the moment allows. Deadlines shrink. Information is incomplete. Emotional stakes rise. Downstream consequences feel opaque. And asking for help seems riskier than improvising.

So the individual adjusts. That adjustment solves the immediate problem, but plants the seed for a future one.

EMOTIONAL LABOR IS THE HIDDEN LOAD

Compensation runs on emotional labor, the unseen effort people expend to manage fear, responsibility, uncertainty, and consequence while still delivering results.

This work rarely appears in dashboards or reports. It doesn't live in systems; it lives in bodies and choices. You notice it in subtle behaviors: the extra check on a step that should be routine, the hesitation to escalate because asking for help feels like admitting incompetence, the decision to push forward despite discomfort because stopping would spark conflict.

Processes almost never account for this load. They assume neutrality, as if every decision were purely technical. But the more consequential the work, the heavier the emotional weight becomes.

That's why identical processes behave differently in different environments. A checklist in a low-stakes setting feels procedural. The same checklist in a context where failure carries human cost becomes something else entirely, a psychological balancing act.

I learned this early in my career during an interview for a role maintaining systems that kept prenatal children alive. The technical challenge didn't intimidate me. The emotional reality did. Knowing that a single mistake could cost a life would have consumed my attention. I could picture myself compensating constantly, second-guessing, overchecking, carrying fear into every decision.

I declined the job, not because I lacked skill, but because I understood my bandwidth. Emotional capacity is finite, and when it's exceeded, behavior shifts. People speed up, slow down, overcorrect, or bypass steps, not out of carelessness, but because the emotional cost of flawless execution feels unbearable.

This is not a side note. Emotional labor is the engine behind compensation. It determines where adjustments happen, how decisions are made, and why processes bend under pressure. Ignore it, and you misread the system entirely.

COMPENSATION BECOMES PATTERN

A single adjustment doesn't break a process. Repetition does.

When the same pressure keeps showing up, the same workaround follows. What starts as improvisation slowly hardens into routine. The exception becomes the norm, and nobody notices the shift because it feels practical.

This is how drift begins, not as a dramatic failure, but as a quiet accumulation of choices that no longer feel temporary. Over time, people stop thinking of the adjustment as a deviation. They start thinking of it as the real way things get done.

At that point, the documented process and the lived process part ways. Not because someone formally changed the rules, but because the adapted version works better under actual conditions.

And with that divergence comes uneven knowledge. The people closest to the work know the real path. New hires learn it through whispers and observation. Adjacent teams remain in the dark. Leadership still points to the official diagram, unaware that it describes a world that no longer exists.

The organization now operates with two processes: the one on paper and the one in practice. They look similar from a distance, but they are not the same.

CAUSAL RECAP BEFORE ESCALATION

Before moving forward, the causal chain needs to be clear. Pressure doesn't arrive evenly, it concentrates in certain places. When that pressure exceeds what the process was designed to handle, people adapt locally to keep work moving. Those adaptations draw heavily on emotional labor. When repeated, they harden into habit. Habit becomes drift.

None of this requires bad intent or incompetence. It's not rebellion, it's structural inevitability when design and reality fall out of alignment.

DRIFT SOLIDIFIES AND BOTTLENECKS APPEAR

Drift is harmless while it stays contained. The risk emerges when it crosses boundaries and begins to shape the system itself.

This is the moment most organizations fail to recognize. They often interpret drift as a lapse in discipline or a training gap. But the real danger appears when drift meets dependency. A process is never a single lane, it's a network of handoffs. And drift doesn't pause at those intersections; it flows through them.

Once a compensated behavior becomes routine, it starts influencing expectations on both ends. Upstream teams assume the adjustment will happen. Downstream teams plan around it. No one names the change, yet everyone relies on it.

At that point, failure stops being occasional. It becomes predictable, occurring in the same places, for the same reasons, every time. And when predictability hardens into constraint, bottlenecks form.

BOTTLENECKS ARE BEHAVIORAL, NOT TECHNICAL

A bottleneck is more than a slowdown, it's a collision point where different interpretations of the same process meet head-on.

Upstream teams act with confidence, following the version of the workflow they've learned through experience. Downstream teams receive outputs that technically break the documented rules but align with what they've come to expect. Systems enforce rigid standards while humans quietly bend them. And accountability often falls on roles that have no control over the conditions that caused the deviation in the first place.

This is the moment drift becomes visible. It rarely announces itself with clarity; instead, it shows up disguised as rework, escalation, delays, or interpersonal friction. Yet the root cause lies further back, the process no longer carries a single shared meaning.

This is why automation alone rarely solves bottlenecks. Speeding up a handoff doesn't resolve the deeper issue: disagreement about what "right" looks like. Technology executes instructions faithfully. People execute what feels safe, practical, and defensible under pressure.

So the bottleneck isn't about capacity. It's about interpretation, a silent divergence that turns coordination into conflict. Until alignment is restored, every fix will treat symptoms, not the disease.

UNSPOKEN EXCEPTIONS BECOME STRUCTURAL DEBT

By the time a bottleneck becomes visible, the real story is already written in silence: unspoken exceptions have taken root.

Every role operates with two sets of rules, the official ones and the private ones. Those private rules emerge because the documented process cannot withstand real-world pressure. Over time, what began as a workaround becomes a norm.

Consider the support agent understands the rule: escalate after five minutes. Yet experience has taught them that escalating too soon before the queue settles draws unwanted attention. Or the compliance analyst who understands the stated threshold yet lowers it because leadership prizes speed. Or the operations supervisor who knows uncertified inputs should be rejected but uses the workaround to keep production alive.

None of these adjustments appear in documentation, yet all of them govern daily reality.

The issue isn't their existence; it's their invisibility. Outsiders never see them. New hires discover them through missteps. Adjacent teams stumble into them as surprises. Systems flag them as errors.

This is how process debt accumulates, not through neglect, but through silence. Every hidden rule adds weight to the system until the official process becomes a fiction and the functional process lives entirely in the shadows.

SKILL VARIABILITY ACCELERATES DRIFT

Drift doesn't spread in a straight line, it accelerates where capability gaps exist.

Most processes are designed for an imagined "average performer," a figure that exists only on paper. Reality looks different: every team is a mix of experience levels, confidence, judgment, and learning speed.

When pressure rises, people fall back on what feels safe. A seasoned employee strips steps to move faster. A newcomer compensates by documenting everything. Someone fluent in the technical details skips safeguards, while a risk-averse colleague adds extra ones.

Each choice makes sense in isolation. Together, they fracture the system. The same task now travels through radically different comfort zones, multiplying variation. Variation breeds unpredictability. Unpredictability turns handoffs into friction points, and friction shows up as delays, rework, and escalation.

Leaders often respond by tightening the screws: more documentation, more approvals, more checkpoints. The intent is stability. The effect is the opposite. Every new control adds weight, increasing pressure on the very people already compensating.

And so the cycle accelerates: pressure rises, compensation expands, drift deepens. What began as adaptation becomes systemic distortion.

EMOTIONAL LOAD SHAPES WHERE BOTTLENECKS FORM

Drift doesn't move evenly through a system, it accelerates wherever capability gaps widen the cracks.

Processes are typically built for an imagined "average performer," a construct that looks neat on paper but doesn't exist in reality. Teams are mosaics of skill levels, confidence, judgment, and learning speed.

When pressure mounts, people retreat to familiar ground. A veteran trims steps to keep momentum. A newcomer compensates with exhaustive documentation. Someone fluent in technical details bypasses safeguards, while a cautious colleague adds extra ones.

Individually, these choices feel rational. Collectively, they splinter the workflow. The same task now travels through wildly different comfort zones, multiplying variation. Variation breeds unpredictability, and unpredictability turns handoffs into friction points, manifesting as delays, rework, and escalation.

Leaders often respond by layering on controls: more documentation, more approvals, more checkpoints. The goal is stability. The outcome is the opposite. Every added control increases weight, amplifying the pressure that triggered compensation in the first place.

And so the cycle accelerates. Pressure rises. Compensation expands. Drift deepens. What began as a practical adjustment evolves into systemic distortion, a process designed for clarity now operating in a fog of improvisation.

DEPARTMENTS CREATE PARALLEL TRUTHS

As drift expands, departments begin shaping their own interpretations of the process. HR frames decisions through the lens of empathy and fairness. Operations focuses on throughput and flow. IT prioritizes logic and consistency. Compliance leans toward risk mitigation and auditability. Frontline roles, meanwhile, make choices that protect stability and survival.

Each perspective makes sense within its own context, but they rarely align. These differences aren't acts of resistance; they're natural responses to local incentives and pressures.

Trouble surfaces when uniformity becomes essential, when timing must synchronize across boundaries, when data needs to reconcile cleanly, or when automation depends on predictable inputs. At that point, the organization isn't running one process anymore. It's running a patchwork of competing truths, stitched together by informal negotiation and quiet compromise.

And where those seams pull tight, bottlenecks appear, not as isolated slowdowns, but as stress points where incompatible interpretations collide.

THE ILLUSION OF CONTROL COLLAPSES

From the leadership vantage point, the breakdown looks sudden, a sharp collapse where stability was assumed. In truth, the fracture has been spreading quietly for months, maybe years.

Executives notice symptoms first: timelines slipping where speed was promised, data misalignments where precision was expected, behaviors that feel like resistance against compliance. The instinctive response is structural, new mandates, fresh tools, reorganized teams. Yet these interventions land on a system that has already rewritten itself in practice.

The official process still exists on paper, but its authority has eroded. What leaders confront is not a failure of discipline; it is the inevitable consequence of designing for an ideal world and then exposing that design to relentless, uneven pressure.

The collapse isn't sudden. It's the final stage of adaptation, a system choosing survival over fidelity long before anyone noticed.

BOTTLENECKS NORMALIZE AND FAILURE BECOMES INVISIBLE

When bottlenecks linger long enough, they stop signaling failure and start feeling like part of the landscape.

This is the most perilous stage of process decay, not because everything looks broken, but because nothing does. The organization learns to work around the friction instead of removing it. Deadlines are met, deliverables ship, and the hidden cost is carried quietly by those closest to the work.

Normalization isn't resolution; it's survival disguised as stability.

THE ORGANIZATION LEARNS TO ROUTE AROUND ITS OWN DESIGN

When bottlenecks become predictable, people stop fighting them and start planning around them. Timelines get padded. Informal checkpoints appear. Work is pre-approved or held back until the "right" moment. Side channels emerge to bypass formal paths entirely.

None of this shows up in documentation, yet it becomes essential knowledge for anyone trying to operate effectively. Over time, the organization learns to route around its own design, creating a shadow system that feels more reliable than the official one.

At this stage, the documented process serves a different purpose. It's no longer the engine of execution, it's the narrative used to justify outcomes after the fact. Real work happens elsewhere: in inboxes, private conversations, and judgment calls that never make it into the system.

This isn't laziness. It's adaptation. People aren't optimizing for compliance; they're optimizing for predictability, because predictability is what keeps the machine running when the design can't.

DATA DECAYS BEFORE ANYONE NOTICES

As work begins to bypass formal systems, the integrity of data erodes, not because people stop caring, but because precision loses its place under pressure.

Information gets entered late, values are estimated, and context disappears. Time stamps no longer reflect reality. Exceptions masquerade as normal, while routine cases are flagged as anomalies. The system still collects data, but what it captures is a shadow of the truth.

This distortion creates a dangerous feedback loop. Dashboards tell a story that no longer matches the lived process. Leadership makes decisions based on representations that lag behind behavior. Interventions target symptoms instead of causes, reinforcing the illusion of control.

Confidence grows even as accuracy declines. The organization becomes certain, and wrong.

This is how failure hides in plain sight: not as chaos, but as a system that looks orderly while quietly drifting away from reality.

ACCOUNTABILITY DETACHES FROM CONTROL

As bottlenecks become routine, accountability begins to migrate, but authority doesn't move with it. Those tasked with delivering results often lack the power to change the conditions that shape them. Metrics are pinned downstream while the root causes remain upstream. Escalations land on roles already stretched thin by constant compensation.

This imbalance doesn't just create stress; it accelerates the cycle. More pressure drives more adaptation, and every adaptation deepens the drift. No one is acting irrationally, the system is simply reinforcing its own logic.

By this stage, familiar remedies fall short. Training can't close the gap. Documentation can't restore alignment. New tools can't untangle what's structural. When design and reality diverge this far, the problem isn't effort, it's behavioral.

PROCESS OWNERSHIP BECOMES SYMBOLIC

When persistent issues refuse to go away, many organizations reach for a familiar solution: assign ownership. A process owner, a steering committee, maybe even a center of excellence.

On paper, this feels like governance. In reality, it often functions as theater. Ownership without insight into the emotional load, the informal shortcuts, and the local incentives shaping behavior cannot reverse drift. The designated owner manages the version of the process that exists in documentation, while the version that actually moves work forward remains untouched.

This disconnect creates an illusion of control. Leadership assumes the process is under management because someone is accountable for it. But accountability here applies to a representation, not the reality. Meanwhile, the real process, the one shaped by pressure and adaptation, continues to evolve quietly, beyond the reach of formal oversight.

WHY AI OFTEN MAKES THIS WORSE

Introducing AI into a fragmented process doesn't restore order, it magnifies what already exists. Algorithms learn from the data they're fed, and that data reflects human adaptation under pressure, not the pristine design leaders imagine.

If shortcuts have become routine, AI will institutionalize them. If escalation has been quietly avoided, AI will normalize the silence. If departments operate with competing interpretations, those inconsistencies will be encoded into the model.

This isn't a failure of AI; it's a failure of inputs. AI cannot tell the difference between intentional design and survival-driven improvisation. It absorbs the system as it is, not as it was meant to be.

Without understanding the human mechanisms that created drift, automation doesn't solve the problem, it accelerates it. AI becomes an amplifier for the very behaviors leadership hoped to correct, turning hidden adaptations into systemic defaults at scale.

FINAL CAUSAL RECAP

Pressure doesn't arrive evenly, it pools in certain places. People adapt to survive it, and those adaptations harden into habits. Habits reshape the process until drift becomes the norm. Drift creates friction, friction turns into bottlenecks, and bottlenecks eventually feel like part of the landscape.

Once failure hides behind normalization, data begins to lie. Dashboards reflect a process that no longer exists, misleading leadership into decisions that add even more pressure. The cycle closes, not as a cautionary tale, but as a description of how work truly behaves under strain.

WHY THIS MATTERS

The purpose of this chapter isn't to dismiss processes, it's to reveal their limits. A process without an understanding of human behavior is only half a system.

People don't break processes; they complete them. They absorb ambiguity, carry risk, and smooth contradictions that no diagram anticipates. They manage emotion in ways no checklist can capture.

When leaders design as if people are interchangeable parts, the structure eventually buckles under the weight of reality. The human system compensates until it can't. But when design accounts for pressure, emotional labor, skill variability, and adaptive judgment, processes gain resilience instead of brittleness.

That's the threshold where leadership begins, not in perfect documentation, but in designing for the way work actually feels.

The next chapter moves closer to that reality. Not in systems or flowcharts, but in the micro-interactions that shape outcomes: the tone of a message, the pause in a conversation, the silence that signals risk.

Because in the end, the inbox, not the workflow diagram, is the real operating system of modern work.

CHAPTER 3

How Organizations Really Think

Most organizations carry an idea about themselves, a polished image that appears in mission statements, slide decks, and the framed values near the entrance. It declares: This is who we are. This is how we work. This is what matters. Leaders echo it in meetings. New employees hear it during onboarding. Consultants treat it as if it were carved in stone.

Yet, anyone who spends real time inside an organization discovers something unsettling: that image rarely matches reality. The way an organization claims to think is not the way it actually operates. Strategy documents describe ideals; daily life reflects adaptation. People don't act according to the official playbook, they act according to what helps them survive.

This chapter explores that hidden space, the gap between formal strategy and the mental model that truly governs behavior. It's the quiet logic shaping choices, influencing culture, and determining outcomes long before any technology or AI initiative enters the scene. If you've ever wondered why identical transformations thrive in one company but fail in another, why AI investments stall despite compelling business cases, or why flawed stories often overpower sound reasoning, the answer lies here: in the unspoken patterns that define how organizations really think.

THE MENTAL MODEL OF A COMPANY

On paper, an organization's mental model looks elegant. Vision shapes strategy. Strategy sets priorities. Priorities inform decisions. Decisions guide behavior. Behavior delivers results. It's a tidy, linear chain that comforts leaders because it implies predictability and control.

Reality is far less orderly.

Vision and strategy do matter, they frame the conversation and signal what leadership claims is important. They define success in theory, and at first, people often believe in that framing. Trusting the system feels natural. Most employees want to believe the story they've been given.

But belief only lasts if it becomes practical. When strategy fails to translate into clear, everyday meaning, what it changes in someone's job, what choices it makes easier or harder, it doesn't become a mental model. It becomes background noise.

Something else fills the gap: the unwritten rules of office life. Cultural shortcuts. Informal norms. Shared assumptions about how decisions really happen. Which risks earn praise and which earn punishment. When speed is celebrated and when caution suddenly becomes the law. These patterns form the lived mental model, the one that actually governs behavior.

And that model is fluid. It shifts with time, leadership changes, and organizational shocks. One year the company believes in bold innovation; the next, it prizes cost control. A new executive arrives, and overnight the rules of survival rewrite themselves. People who have endured a few of these cycles learn quickly: strategy is temporary, survival is not.

So they adapt. They stop anchoring decisions to official intent and start anchoring them to observed reality. What happens when we push for X? Who takes the fall when Y fails? Which initiatives vanish quietly after six months? This isn't cynicism, it's pattern recognition. It's cognition under uncertainty.

The true mental model of an organization isn't what leaders declare. It's what experience teaches. Every meeting, every reward, every quiet retreat from a bold promise adds another layer to that model. And until leaders understand this gap, the space between stated strategy and lived reality, they will keep wondering why logic loses to stories, why transformations stall, and why the same plan thrives in one place but collapses in another.

ORGANIZATIONS ARE COGNITIVE SYSTEMS

Once you recognize this dynamic, it becomes clear that organizations cannot be understood as rigid structures or mechanical systems. They do not simply execute plans like machines. They operate as cognitive ecosystems, living networks of perception and interpretation.

Groups form beliefs much like individuals do: through repeated experiences, reinforcement, trust, and shared stories. Logic alone rarely wins. A strategy document may outline what the company values, but belief emerges from something deeper, leadership credibility, peer influence, and the emotional tone of daily life. When trust in leadership is strong, people lean into its narrative. When trust falters, those narratives are filtered, reshaped, or quietly discarded.

Mission statements and corporate values matter, but mostly as an opening signal. They set the stage for new hires and frame expectations. Yet that influence lasts only until reality either validates or contradicts the promise. Belief is not sustained by words; it is sustained by experience.

The real formation of belief happens in relationships, during moments of pressure, shared challenges, and candid conversations when the stakes feel real. These interactions are intimate. They build trust or erode it. And trust is the currency that determines whether a story becomes a conviction or fades into noise.

Every individual brings a personal history into this mix, past experiences, cultural assumptions, and beliefs about authority and safety. These personal frameworks collide and converge, creating a social process where some interpretations spread while others disappear. Group belief is not commanded; it emerges.

This complexity has deepened in recent years. External narratives, shaped by social media, cultural debates, and global events, flow into organizations constantly. Employees interpret company messages through the lens of what they see and hear outside. Sometimes these external signals reinforce internal intent; other times they undermine it completely.

The result is a cognitive landscape that is fragmented, layered, and always in motion. Leaders often assume they control this process, but in truth, their influence is partial and fragile. Understanding this reality is not optional, it is the starting point for any leader who hopes to shape belief rather than chase it.

WHY LOGIC LOSES TO SOCIAL REALITY

One of the most enduring frustrations in organizational change is this: even when the case for change is flawless, nothing moves. You can present the cost of inefficiency in stark detail, calculate wasted hours, and model opportunity loss down to the last dollar. Leaders nod. They agree. And yet, behavior stays the same.

This isn't because people are irrational. It's because logic collides with identity. In many organizations, culture has calcified around the phrase, "This is how we've always done it." That phrase isn't about process, it's about safety. Familiar routines feel survivable. Altering them, even for good reason, introduces uncertainty. And uncertainty is emotionally expensive.

When leaders see the true cost of entrenched behaviors, they're often stunned. The numbers are compelling. The analysis is clear. But clarity doesn't guarantee action. Agreement rarely translates into momentum.

Change only happens when people are motivated to think differently, and motivation is rarely born from numbers alone. Despite the rhetoric of being "data-driven," most organizations run on vision, not metrics. KPIs serve as destinations, not engines. A target like "20 percent improvement" is abstract. What matters is the story behind that target, the meaning of the journey and whether it feels purposeful or threatening.

Here's the paradox: many metrics are invented. Someone chose a number and declared it significant. People sense this. They don't attach emotionally to the metric itself; they attach to the narrative surrounding it. Numbers may inform decisions, but stories inspire action.

What employees want, often quietly, is purpose. They want to believe their effort matters, that someone cares, that the work connects to something human, not just something efficient. Shared narrative provides that sense of meaning. Logic doesn't.

So when a rational argument collides with a story that offers identity, belonging, or safety, logic almost always loses. Not because it's wrong, but because it's incomplete. Change is never just a technical exercise; it's a cognitive and emotional one. Until leaders grasp that truth, they'll keep wondering why airtight business cases fail to move the needle.

WHAT LEADERS BELIEVE VERSUS WHAT EMPLOYEES BELIEVE

This is where the gap becomes visible, and dangerous. Leaders often assume the organization shares their perspective. They see alignment reflected in formal artifacts: the strategy deck, the operating model, the governance framework. On paper, everything looks synchronized.

But employees navigate a different reality. Their beliefs are shaped by experience, not intention. They know which leaders deliver and which ones don't. They've learned which risks are rewarded and which quietly end careers. They recognize which initiatives drive real change and which are little more than theater.

Neither side is wrong; they're simply looking through different lenses. Leadership tends to imagine culture as a single, unified system. Employees experience it as layered and fragmented, leadership culture, team culture, departmental culture. These layers intersect but rarely align perfectly.

Each layer carries its own architecture of norms and assumptions, and individuals live at the crossroads of several at once. That's why culture cannot be repaired with slogans or polished statements. It isn't ornamental. It's structural. It bears weight, and when ignored, it cracks.

CULTURE AS A BEHAVIORAL FORCE

Culture becomes powerful when belief hardens into instinct. Over time, every department develops its own reflexes, automatic responses shaped by its mission and survival logic. These reflexes make sense within each silo. But when they collide, friction becomes inevitable.

Take Finance. Its purpose is risk protection, so caution becomes second nature. Over years, that instinct turns into a reflex to slow decisions, tighten controls, and demand exhaustive proof. What begins as prudence morphs into paralysis. Momentum dies under the weight of spreadsheets, and other teams feel like they're forever pitching uphill.

Marketing operates on a different clock. Attention and novelty are its lifeblood. The reflex? Move fast, capture signal, figure out the rest later. The shadow side is chaos, shiny-object syndrome, forgotten processes, and cleanup deferred until someone else pays the price.

Sales runs on the scoreboard. Winning matters most. The reflex is to say yes, close the deal at any cost. Dysfunction follows: inflated promises, custom terms, impossible timelines, and features that don't exist yet. The organization inherits the debt.

IT, tasked with stability and security, defaults to caution. Over time, that caution becomes gatekeeping disguised as rigor. Change slows. Shadow systems appear. IT clamps down harder, and the cycle repeats.

HR plays therapist and referee. Its reflex is containment, keep the peace, manage the fires. The dysfunction? Endless firefighting while strategic culture work gets postponed indefinitely.

None of this is malicious. It's human. Each specialization develops coping mechanisms that eventually harden into identity. And when those identities collide, the organization pays the tax, in time, trust, and energy.

Once you see these patterns, dysfunction stops feeling mysterious. You can predict the argument before the meeting even begins. Finance will ask for proof. Marketing will push for speed. Sales will promise the moon. IT will tighten the gates. HR will try to keep everyone calm. It's not chaos, it's choreography. And unless leaders learn to rewrite the reflexes, the dance never changes.

WHY THE SAME TOOL SUCCEEDS IN ONE TEAM AND FAILS IN ANOTHER

This is the fault line where many transformation efforts collapse. A single tool, deployed across two teams, can produce radically different results. One group adopts it enthusiastically; another resists or misuses it. Leaders point to poor adoption. Vendors cite weak change management. Everyone blames execution.

The truth is both simpler and more uncomfortable: every tool enters a belief system.

Teams don't just use technology, they interpret it. They filter it through their mental models, their reflexes, and their assumptions about risk, control, and value. A tool is never neutral; it inherits the culture it touches.

Consider AI. Introduced first to Finance, it will likely be framed as a compliance engine, a mechanism for tightening oversight and reducing discretion. Other teams watch and conclude: AI equals control. Introduced first to Sales, the same technology becomes a speed accelerator, a way to close deals faster and push boundaries. Now the signal is different: AI equals velocity. Both interpretations ripple outward, shaping trust and tension.

Uneven rollout doesn't just create inconsistency, it amplifies existing dysfunction. If an organization struggles with internal friction, AI will magnify it. Technology doesn't erase cultural fault lines; it deepens them.

This is why systematic rollout plans often fail. Human systems don't adapt cleanly under pressure. Forcing adoption produces two outcomes: outright rejection or shallow compliance that masks deeper resistance. Neither creates transformation.

AI doesn't fix behavior. It mirrors it. It reflects the stories, habits, and survival patterns already in place. Until leaders address those patterns, every new tool will simply become another artifact of the old system.

HOW AI INTERACTS WITH COLLECTIVE MENTAL MODELS

When AI brings clarity into an organization, the first reaction is rarely excitement, it's fear. Fear of being replaced. Fear of being exposed. Fear of losing relevance. Those fears quickly harden into protective narratives: AI is overhyped. AI isn't ready. AI doesn't understand what we do. These stories aren't about technology; they're about survival.

The challenge often isn't AI's capability, it's how the conversation begins. Most discussions frame AI in technical terms: features, architecture, abstract possibilities. That language feels distant and intimidating, which only amplifies anxiety. People fear what they don't understand.

Fear begins to fade when AI is explained in human terms. Break it down by what it imitates well and where it struggles. Translate those traits into familiar equivalents. Suddenly, AI looks less like an inscrutable force and more like a junior colleague, eager, capable in some areas, but in need of guidance and boundaries. That metaphor matters. Everyone understands how learning works: deliberate instruction, natural guardrails, gradual development over time.

When AI is framed this way, something shifts. People start asking where it helps and where it doesn't. Curiosity replaces resistance.

The most successful adoption doesn't start with sweeping enterprise platforms. It starts small, with relevance at the micro level. Sit with someone in their actual workflow. Find the spot where time evaporates. Show how AI can turn a fifteen-minute grind into a one-minute click. That moment changes everything: This matters. This helps. The narrative flips.

And when the narrative flips, it spreads. People talk. Success stories circulate informally. Belief begins to shift. The mental architecture of the organization rewires itself, not because of a mandate, but because the experience feels real and useful.

AI adoption isn't about dazzling features or grand promises. It's about reframing fear into familiarity and turning abstract potential into tangible relief. That's where transformation begins.

CULTURE IS THE ARCHITECTURE BENEATH THE ARCHITECTURE

Culture is not decoration, it's the framework that carries the weight of everything else. Organizations aren't simple hierarchies; they're networks of overlapping architectures: individuals, teams, departments, and the enterprise as a whole. These layers don't stack neatly. They intersect, accumulate, and travel with people as they move through the system.

Each layer has its own cultural logic, and those logics coexist rather than dissolve. When leaders talk about culture, they often choose a single lens, employee engagement, leadership values, workplace norms. Each perspective is valid, but none tells the full story.

AI doesn't interact with one layer; it touches all of them at once. It applies pressure across the entire structure, revealing every weak joint. Introducing AI isn't just a technical deployment, it's a behavioral shift. If the underlying architecture isn't prepared, the risk isn't mechanical. It's human. And human risk is harder to patch.

SIGNALS OF STRENGTH AND BRITTLENESS

Here's the hard truth: no organization is fully prepared for AI, no matter what the slide decks claim. Readiness isn't a finish line you cross, it's a path you travel.

The organizations that thrive over time share one trait: they understand their human limits. They know transformation isn't instant. They measure success by shifts in behavior, not by the speed of system deployment. Instead of forcing adoption everywhere, they start where the impact feels real and the fear is low. They let belief spread through experience, not mandate.

They also embrace imperfection. Culture never freezes in place. Tension never vanishes. But with patience, a baseline of stability can form.

Watch for early warning signs: overconfidence, aggressive rollouts, and an obsession with tools instead of people. The strongest indicator of resilience isn't technical sophistication, it's humility. The willingness to observe, listen, and learn before acting. That mindset turns readiness from illusion into progress.

DETECTING INVISIBLE BELIEFS

The most demanding work for leaders isn't technical, it's perceptual. You can't uncover hidden beliefs in others until you've examined your own. Many operate on inherited assumptions rather than tested convictions. They hold what they were taught, not what they've questioned.

Detecting belief follows a familiar rhythm: listening deeply, observing patterns, noticing what isn't said, and checking your own bias along the way. Leaders already form judgments about their people, but accuracy is fragile, and bias is persistent.

Unspoken beliefs leave traces in language: in emails, meeting notes, and documentation. AI will amplify whatever is encoded there. The more unconscious the belief, the greater the risk of distortion. What feels invisible today becomes systemic tomorrow.

In an AI-driven world, leadership isn't about tightening control, it's about sharpening perception. It means seeing the organization as it truly operates, not as the slide deck claims. The question isn't "What do we believe?" but "What beliefs are shaping behavior beneath the surface?"

THE SOCIAL PHYSICS OF WORK

Organizations aren't engineered machines running on pure logic; they're living social systems shaped by belief, identity, and story. Behavior builds culture, and culture drives results. AI doesn't rewrite that dynamic, it simply throws light on it.

To achieve predictable outcomes, you must grasp how organizations truly think, not in theory but in practice. This is the work beneath the work.

CHAPTER 4

The Behavioral Economy of Work

WHY PEOPLE DO WHAT THEY DO

In nearly every organization, there comes a moment when someone stares at a workflow, a dashboard, a policy, or a new system rollout and wonders:

What's really going on here?

Why do employees bypass the official process? Why rush when precision is critical? Why push back against tools that seem objectively better? Why stay silent in meetings only to vent later? And why does every report glow green while the team feels like they're drowning?

These questions often surface with frustration, sometimes disbelief, and occasionally judgment. Beneath them lurks an assumption: the issue must be ignorance, laziness, incompetence, resistance to change, or a bad attitude.

That assumption is almost always wrong.

What appears inefficient from the outside often makes perfect sense internally, once you understand what people are optimizing for. The disconnect happens because leaders, architects, and transformation teams tend to measure behavior against the wrong yardstick. They look through the lens of process efficiency, technical capability, or strategic intent. But employees aren't operating in that economy.

They're navigating a different one, a behavioral economy.

This isn't abstract theory or leadership jargon. It's something you can observe, anticipate, and design for, if you're willing to stop moralizing behavior and start decoding it.

Here's the principle that changes everything:

Every workflow is a transaction.

Every habit earns a paycheck.

Every inefficiency persists because it pays someone back in some way.

When you uncover what people are being shielded from, or what they're being compensated to avoid, the mystery evaporates. Behavior becomes predictable.

The truth is, people rarely resist change for the sake of resistance. They resist because the current system protects them from risk, embarrassment, overload, or failure. They cling to workarounds because those shortcuts buy them time, autonomy, or peace of mind. What looks like chaos is often a carefully negotiated survival strategy.

If you want transformation to stick, you can't just design for the technical economy. You have to design for the behavioral one, the hidden marketplace where every action has a price and every inefficiency is currency.

INCENTIVES ARE NOT REWARDS. THEY ARE RISK.

When most organizations talk about incentives, the conversation usually centers on bonuses, performance ratings, promotions, or penalties. Those elements matter, but they're not what truly shapes everyday decisions.

In this book, the term incentive refers to something far more basic: any factor, whether stated or implied, that alters how much personal, emotional, reputational, or cognitive risk someone feels when choosing between two actions.

This definition is critical because it explains why so many workplace behaviors appear irrational, until you see them through the lens of self-preservation.

Every day, employees run a silent cost-benefit analysis. It's not written in spreadsheets or articulated in meetings. It happens in feelings, almost instinctively:

Is this safe?

Will I look incompetent?

Could this spark conflict?

Will it expose me?

Will it slow me down or put me at odds with my manager?

Does this threaten my identity as someone who knows what they're doing?

These questions hum beneath nearly every choice, from a minor workaround to a major leadership decision.

Once you grasp this, so-called "bad behavior" starts to look remarkably logical. People aren't sabotaging systems or resisting change for sport, they're protecting themselves from risk, embarrassment, overload, or loss of credibility. What seems inefficient is often the safest route in the economy they're operating in: the behavioral economy.

If you want to influence behavior, you can't just adjust bonuses or penalties. You have to understand the invisible incentives, the ones that trade in security, identity, and trust.

STAYING LATE AS A CURRENCY

One of the most common behaviors in organizations is deceptively simple: staying late.

It's rarely questioned because it carries a powerful signal. When someone is online after hours, answering emails at midnight, or visible long past closing time, the message is clear, this person is committed. They're dependable. They care.

That perception creates a strong incentive. But beneath the surface, what does this habit really accomplish?

Often, it acts as a cover. Extra hours can conceal poor prioritization, vague objectives, and broken delivery cycles. Instead of addressing systemic inefficiencies, the organization transfers the burden to individuals, who absorb the pain through personal sacrifice.

From a behavioral perspective, this is entirely rational. Staying late feels safer than challenging scope or admitting deadlines are unrealistic. It sidesteps uncomfortable conversations and shields the employee from appearing incapable. In the short term, it buys security, even if the long-term cost is burnout and unsustainable norms.

The reason this persists is simple: it pays a psychological salary. That salary might come in the form of approval, reassurance, or the comfort of maintaining an identity as "the reliable one." As long as those rewards remain intact, the behavior will endure, regardless of how often leaders champion balance or warn about exhaustion.

The real question isn't why people stay late. It's what invisible economy makes that choice feel safer than fixing the system.

AGREEMENT AS SELF-PROTECTION

One of the most persistent incentives appears in meetings. People nod along. They agree, or at least pretend to. They stay quiet and let the conversation move forward.

From the outside, this looks like alignment. Leaders often interpret silence as consensus: "No questions? Perfect. Everyone's aligned." But silence is rarely neutral.

More often, it's a shield. Behind it sits fear, fear of sounding uninformed, irritating a senior leader, or being branded as difficult. Fear of slowing progress. Fear of consequences that ripple beyond the meeting.

In that context, withholding questions feels safer than speaking up. It preserves relationships, avoids friction, and protects identity. Agreeing, or appearing to agree, becomes a survival tactic.

The irony is striking: what leaders read as maturity or competence is often a signal that the environment isn't safe enough for clarity. When silence becomes the norm, problems surface late, decisions rest on shaky assumptions, and accountability blurs.

Yet from the individual's perspective, the choice is rational. It minimizes immediate risk. It buys security. And like any habit that pays a psychological salary, approval, safety, belonging, it persists, no matter how many times leaders say, "We want honest feedback."

The question isn't why people stay quiet. It's what invisible economy makes silence feel like the smartest move in the room.

THE WORST DECISION IS OFTEN NO DECISION

Nowhere is the hidden incentive more visible than in leadership. One of the most damaging patterns isn't a poor decision, it's the absence of one.

For many leaders, inaction feels like the safest move. If nothing is decided, nothing can be wrong. Delay seems prudent. Requesting more data sounds responsible. And sometimes, that caution is justified. But repeated over time, it becomes avoidance disguised as diligence.

What often goes unnoticed is that indecision is not neutral. It carries weight. It creates ambiguity, pushes risk downstream, and forces teams to improvise in the dark. Work slows, fragments, or stalls entirely, not because the team lacks skill, but because direction never arrived.

Leadership exists to absorb risk, not deflect it. When leaders hesitate indefinitely, the cost doesn't vanish; it shifts. Teams pay in confusion, wasted effort, and mounting frustration.

Why does this persist? Because the short-term rewards are seductive. Few leaders are penalized for waiting. Asking for more information sounds thoughtful, even strategic. In reality, it often serves as a shield, a way to avoid being wrong, avoid owning consequences, and avoid exposure.

The incentive is clear: indecision feels safe. And until organizations stop treating hesitation as harmless, leaders will continue to choose it.

The question isn't whether leaders make bad calls. It's whether the system makes standing still look wiser than moving forward.

SPEED OVER CORRECTNESS

Speed has become one of the most dominant, and least visible, incentives inside modern organizations. Delivery metrics, throughput targets, and looming deadlines create an environment where urgency isn't an exception; it's the default.

In that climate, accuracy feels expensive. It demands time, coordination, and scrutiny, all of which slow momentum. So people adapt. They cut corners, accept imperfect solutions, and prioritize finishing over refining. From the outside, this looks reckless. From the inside, it feels like survival.

Consider the reality most teams face: constant overload, fragmented attention, and what I call "drive-bys", last-minute requests, urgent pings, escalations that hijack focus. These interruptions rarely appear in official process maps, yet they dominate the actual workday.

When formal systems fail to account for these pressures, employees build their own. They track tasks in personal spreadsheets, create shadow workflows, and accumulate exceptions until the unofficial process becomes the real one. Over time, these adaptations harden into habits, layering an invisible operating system on top of the official one.

Why does speed win? Because it lowers immediate risk. Moving fast avoids scrutiny and keeps leaders happy in the short term. Correctness, on the other hand, raises risk, it slows progress, invites debate, and exposes gaps.

Unless leaders deliberately rebalance that trade-off, making accuracy as safe and rewarding as speed, the behavioral economy will keep favoring shortcuts. And the organization will continue to run on a patchwork of informal systems designed for survival, not sustainability.

FAMILIARITY BEATS "BETTER"

One of the biggest frustrations in modernization efforts is the pushback against new tools. Leaders often ask, "We gave them something better, why won't they use it?"

That question hides an assumption: people choose tools because they're objectively superior. In reality, they don't. They choose what feels familiar, what gives them control, and what fits the rhythm of their actual workday.

Most employees aren't sitting around evaluating options. They're stretched thin, juggling deadlines, and trying to survive the week. In that context, a new tool doesn't look like progress, it looks like risk. It threatens competence, introduces uncertainty, and demands learning time they don't have.

If the tool was designed without their input, the problem deepens. It feels imposed, disconnected from reality, and foreign to the way work really happens. So people stick with what they know, not because it's the best option, but because it's the safest.

Here's the interesting part: when you give people space to talk about their work without fear, everything changes. Decades of frustration surface. People who've been in the role for twenty years and those who've been there for one react the same way, the only difference is how much history they carry.

Frontline employees hold some of the richest operational knowledge in any organization. Yet that knowledge is often ignored until something breaks, and suddenly leaders scramble to understand how things actually work.

Listening to those employees isn't just about gathering requirements. It's emotional decompression. It's validation. It's trust-building. And trust is the currency of adoption.

People don't need every suggestion implemented. They need to know their voice matters. When that happens, resistance fades and adoption accelerates, not because the tool changed, but because the behavioral economy did.

FEAR, SAFETY, AND THE NEED TO BELONG

Fear isn't a defect, it's data. It signals something important.

Employees worry about losing their jobs, becoming irrelevant, making mistakes, or being exposed. These fears aren't theoretical; they're anchored in real human needs, income, identity, dignity, belonging.

For many, especially those in long-tenured roles, change feels threatening because of how they were trained. They were taught to execute, not to question. Over time, the task becomes the identity. So when the task changes, it feels like they are under attack.

This is why sweeping transformations often fail. They overwhelm. They spike perceived risk. People retreat into behaviors that feel safe.

Sustainable change works differently. It happens in increments, micro-adjustments that allow people to adapt without losing their sense of self.

Trust is the foundation. People can live with imperfect decisions if they believe the intent was honest and the principles were clear. What they cannot tolerate is duplicity, leaders saying one thing while rewarding another.

Once trust fractures, it spreads quickly. Silence replaces dialogue. People stop raising concerns. They disengage. And when that happens, no amount of process redesign or technology rollout will fix the culture underneath.

Fear isn't the enemy. Ignoring what it's telling you is.

PSYCHOLOGICAL SAFETY IS NOT SOFT. IT IS STRUCTURAL

Psychological safety is often dismissed as a cultural extra, something nice to have once the "real work" is finished. In truth, it's the foundation for adoption and engagement. Without it, compliance becomes performative. People nod, agree, and attend training, but their real behaviors drift elsewhere.

This is why adoption rarely fails because of poor training. It fails because of weak relationships. Rolling out a tool without understanding the people who will use it is like overselling on a first date, you push too hard, and the other person pulls away.

Every rollout sends a signal, whether leaders notice it or not. It tells employees what the organization values, trust, respect, and intent, or the lack of it. When that signal feels heavy-handed, resistance grows. Punishment may seem like control, but it doesn't scale; it corrodes culture and eventually harms the business. Employees aren't disposable components. They're layered investments, and when those layers are ignored, people retreat into behaviors designed for self-protection.

This dynamic doesn't stop with tools. It applies to AI as well. AI isn't neutral. It comes with blind spots, constraints, and limitations. Treating it as flawless or autonomous introduces new risks. Ironically, over-trusting AI is often a fear response, a way to dodge responsibility.

AI doesn't eliminate accountability; it redistributes it. Leaders who fail to grasp that shift will be blindsided by the consequences.

Psychological safety isn't a luxury. It's the operating system for change. Without it, every transformation, digital or human, runs on borrowed time.

BEHAVIORAL OPTIMIZATION IS NOT CONTROL

Behavioral optimization is often mistaken for manipulation or rigid compliance. In reality, it's something entirely different.

It's about shaping an environment where judgment is encouraged, not suppressed, where autonomy exists within clear boundaries, and where purpose is visible rather than buried in jargon. It's about creating spaces where asking questions signals strength, not risk.

Before introducing tools designed to change behavior, leaders must first understand the behavior itself. Adoption doesn't start with technology; it starts with trust. And trust is built through understanding, an understanding that takes time, observation, and genuine engagement.

Generic training rarely delivers adoption because it speaks to everyone and resonates with no one. Relevance is role-specific. People need to see how a tool fits their job, their temperament, and the reality of their day-to-day work. Without that connection, they'll comply on the surface while clinging to legacy habits behind the scenes.

This truth becomes even sharper with AI. Its theoretical potential is vast, but potential means nothing if employees can't answer one simple question: What does this mean for me?

Persona-level insight is critical. What does this role actually do? Why is it done that way? What pressures shape those choices? What risks are they managing every hour? Until those questions are answered, AI remains a demo, a shiny presentation, not a working capability.

Behavioral optimization isn't about control. It's about alignment, between tools, trust, and the human realities that make organizations run.

WHEN AI ENTERS A BEHAVIORALLY OPTIMIZED ENVIRONMENT

In organizations that have invested in behavioral maturity, AI adoption feels less like a mandate and more like an invitation. It isn't imposed; it's explored.

Employees approach AI as an additional tool, something worth testing, something that might relieve them of repetitive tasks and return precious time. That mindset only emerges when critical thinking is treated as core work, not an after-hours luxury.

Professional development and critical thinking are often conflated, but they serve different purposes. Learning new skills expands capability; thinking critically reshapes how work is done. Most organizations fund the first and neglect the second, starving the very space where innovation grows.

When people have room to reflect, experiment, and question assumptions, AI shifts from threat to catalyst. It becomes a partner in progress rather than a symbol of disruption.

Will everyone embrace it? No. Enthusiasm will vary. But culture outweighs individual energy. A culture that rewards curiosity and exploration will uncover value, even if adoption starts unevenly.

AI thrives where thinking thrives. Without that foundation, it remains a shiny demo. With it, it becomes a lever for transformation.

HOW LEADERS REINFORCE THE WRONG INCENTIVES

Most leaders don't wake up intending to create dysfunctional cultures. Yet many do, by accident.

The moment a scoreboard is chosen, incentives are set. Metrics become magnets for behavior, whether leaders intend it or not. What gets measured, praised, funded, and tolerated quietly becomes the real rulebook. Vision statements may inspire, but they don't govern. Metrics do.

And people don't optimize for lofty language; they optimize for safety. When delivery dates, feature counts, or adoption numbers are tracked as proxies, those proxies quickly replace the outcomes they were meant to represent.

There's another layer leaders often underestimate: translation. Messages don't arrive intact. They morph into survival rules at the team level:

What can I say without risk?

What should I hide?

What gets rewarded?

What gets me in trouble?

When urgency earns praise and uncertainty earns punishment, confidence becomes theater. Dashboards turn green even when reality is anything but. Risk doesn't vanish, it goes underground.

Then pressure mounts. Teams adapt. They cut unmeasured work, chase visible wins, and celebrate last-minute rescues. Leadership applauds those heroics, funds them, and promotes the saviors. The loop closes:

Pressure → Adaptation → Visible success → Reward.

Over time, the pattern hardens: outputs over outcomes, speed over safety, heroics over prevention, visibility over truth. And when VIPs bypass process, the real rule becomes clear: power beats policy.

AI amplifies this dynamic. It's easy to produce something impressive, a slick demo, a flashy prototype. It's far harder to operationalize AI safely. Yet leaders often reward the demo, not the discipline.

The damage isn't a single bad call; it's systemic erosion. Rework loops multiply. Quality debt grows. Burnout spreads. Shadow processes emerge. Adoption becomes theater. Trust evaporates, first in reports, then in leadership reactions. Eventually, everyone starts managing optics instead of reality.

The fix isn't asking people to "try harder." The fix is rewriting the scoreboard.

Reward speed with stability, not speed alone.

Reward adoption with outcomes, not logins.

Reward early risk surfacing, not late heroics.

Reward calibrated confidence, not loud certainty.

And with AI, the boring work matters most: evaluation, groundedness, training, telemetry, ownership, incident learning. Make invisible work visible. Bake change management, support load, data readiness, governance controls, rollback plans, and operational health into the definition of done.

If you only count the launch, you teach the organization that everything after launch is optional. And optional work is the first thing to disappear under pressure.

Culture isn't shaped by slogans. It's shaped by scoreboards. Change the scoreboard, and you change the game.

THE HUMAN COST OF REMOVING HUMANS

There's one last misconception worth dismantling: the belief that systems will eventually replace people entirely. In this imagined future, work runs without facilitators, without questions, without emotion, just flawless execution.

It's an appealing fantasy: AI following instructions perfectly, free of friction. But reality doesn't cooperate.

When AI misfires, who carries the accountability? When outcomes diverge from expectations, who owns the result? When oversight becomes constant, who shoulders the burden of supervision?

Humans bring something AI cannot replicate, intuition, lived experience, and contextual judgment. AI operates on systematic knowledge; humans navigate nuance. Anyone who has worked with generative AI knows this firsthand. Give a skilled human a vague brief, and they infer intent almost instantly. Give the same brief to AI, and you'll repeat, clarify, and reframe endlessly.

Removing human layers doesn't erase complexity; it simply moves it. And if leaders fail to anticipate that shift, they won't eliminate problems, they'll exchange them for a new set, often more costly and harder to manage.

AI can accelerate work, but it cannot replace the human capacity for sense-making. The question isn't whether humans disappear, it's how organizations design systems where technology amplifies judgment instead of pretending to replace it.

DESIGNING THE EXCHANGE

Culture isn't defined by what leaders say in town halls or write in vision statements. It's revealed in the choices people make when priorities collide.

Those choices aren't random. Sometimes they're about job security. Sometimes about credibility. Often they're tied to identity, belonging, pride, or purpose, and usually, it's a mix of all of these.

Culture is the accumulated pattern of how people resolve risk and expectation in real situations, not in aspirational language. Leaders rarely get the culture they imagine. They get the culture their incentives, pressures, and tolerances make possible.

AI doesn't rewrite that truth, it magnifies it. Introducing AI isn't just adding a tool; it's inserting a system that changes visibility, pace, comparison, and accountability inside an already complex human ecosystem.

If incentives are unclear or misaligned, the system will still learn, but not from vision statements. It will learn from behavior. And what it learns will mirror the real trade-offs people navigate every day, not the ones leaders assume exist.

That's why understanding the behavioral economy of work is no longer optional. It's foundational. Without it, transformations look sleek on the surface but remain fragile underneath.

Once you understand the exchange, the hidden calculus behind every choice, behavior stops feeling chaotic. It becomes legible. Predictable. And when behavior is predictable, it becomes designable.

Not through control or mandates, but by reshaping the risks people carry, the safety they feel, and the invisible costs they absorb or avoid.

Culture isn't a slogan. It's a system of exchanges. And in the age of AI, those exchanges are accelerating. The question isn't whether you can control them, it's whether you can design conditions where the right behaviors feel like the safest ones.

Data is Human Before it is Technical

WHY DEFINITIONS ARE THE BATTLEFIELD

Many organizations assume their data challenges emerge late in the process, somewhere inside the machinery of analytics. They picture the trouble lurking in the warehouse, the dashboard, the integration layer, the vendor contract, or the pipeline. When reports conflict, when metrics refuse to align, when leaders debate which chart reflects reality, the instinct is predictable: repair the technology. Swap the tool. Upgrade the platform. Add AI.

That instinct feels reasonable because it feels familiar. Technology is visible. It can be bought, installed, and showcased. It offers the comfort of control. If the issue looks technical, the fix seems achievable.

Yet this assumption is almost always wrong.

The most stubborn data problems rarely begin with systems. They begin with people. Long before a record enters a database, it has already been shaped by human judgment, by interpretation, incentives, fears, and organizational context. By the time data becomes "technical," the most influential decisions about its meaning have already been made, often without notice.

Data is human first, technical second.

This truth unsettles because it challenges a quiet organizational belief: that data is neutral, objective, and capable of settling disputes. Leaders want data to serve as a stabilizer, a solid anchor that eliminates uncertainty. But ambiguity does not vanish when its source is human.

Every metric exists because someone cared enough to capture it. Someone observed an event and decided it mattered. Someone chose to record it, define it, categorize it, and determine who could access it. Someone imagined how it might later justify a decision. These choices are not trivial; they reflect the lived reality of the organization.

They are shaped by roles and responsibilities, by pressure and accountability, by fear and survival instincts. They emerge from what happens when things go wrong, who gets blamed, who gets questioned, who remains protected.

This is why most disputes over data are not really about precision. They are about interpretation. And interpretation, inside any organization, is inseparable from power.

Definitions become the terrain where these battles play out. They are not mere semantics; they are negotiations over authority, influence, and control. When two teams argue over what "revenue" means, they are not debating vocabulary, they are defending priorities, budgets, and reputations.

Technology cannot resolve this tension because the tension is not technical. It is cultural. It is political. It is human.

So when organizations rush to modernize platforms or inject AI into their analytics stack, they often miss the deeper issue: the meaning of data is forged long before the system ever touches it. Until that reality is acknowledged, new tools will only mask old disagreements.

The question worth asking is not "Which dashboard is correct?" but "Whose perspective shaped the numbers we see?" Because behind every data point lies a chain of decisions, decisions that reveal values, fears, and rewards.

And that is why the real work of data is not just data wrangling. It is negotiating meaning. It is confronting the human forces that define what counts as truth.

HOW DEFINITION BATTLES BEGIN

Definition disputes rarely announce themselves as battles. They begin quietly, disguised as shared understanding. Two people use the same term and assume alignment. A report circulates without challenge. A dashboard becomes routine. A metric is quoted in a meeting, and heads nod in agreement. On the surface, everything looks synchronized.

That harmony is fragile. It lasts only until reality forces a test.

The first cracks are subtle. Someone wonders why their figure doesn't match another team's. A colleague blames timing. A third group points to a different source. Everyone treats it as temporary, a glitch, a technical hiccup, something that can be patched.

This belief lingers because questioning meaning feels risky. It slows progress. It introduces tension. It demands conversations few are rewarded for having.

But the pattern repeats. Discrepancies return. Explanations lose their power. Arguments resurface in new forms. Eventually, the realization lands: the math isn't broken. The interpretation is.

Words that sound solid, urgent, priority, complete, compliant, successful, are anything but. Their meaning stretches and bends under pressure. "Urgent" depends on who speaks and who listens. "Priority" shifts with incentives. "Done" changes depending on whether speed, accuracy, compliance, or optics matter most.

Organizations try to tame this elasticity. They publish glossaries, codify rules, and document expectations. Yet those definitions rarely survive real-world stress.

When stakes rise, language becomes a shield. People adapt definitions to protect themselves, to match how they're measured, judged, and held accountable. This isn't sabotage; it's survival.

The goal isn't to undermine governance. It's to avoid risk, sidestep blame, and keep momentum. Meaning is renegotiated constantly, long before any system enforces it.

That's why interpretation happens upstream, before data enters a platform. Attention becomes the first enforcement mechanism: what gets noticed, escalated, deferred, or ignored determines what becomes "real."

Technology doesn't correct this dynamic. It hardcodes it. Systems don't neutralize human behavior, they preserve it in digital form.

WHY MEANING IS POLITICAL

Meaning is never passive. It doesn't just describe reality, it shapes it.

When you define a term, you're not simply labeling something. You're setting expectations. You're signaling what matters and what doesn't. You're influencing priorities and directing behavior. In doing so, you decide, often quietly, who will face scrutiny and who will remain protected.

That's why definitions carry political weight, whether anyone admits it or not.

A metric isn't just a measurement. It's a lens. It frames the story of performance, determines which questions get asked, and dictates what qualifies as success versus what gets dismissed as irrelevant. Whoever owns the definition owns the narrative.

This is why teams cling to their version of a metric. Metrics are not neutral, they are identity markers. They reveal how a department sees its role, the risks it shoulders, and the logic behind its decisions.

Consider the contrasts:

Finance prioritizes precision because errors invite regulatory and audit exposure.

Operations values speed because delays threaten revenue and customer trust.

HR emphasizes consistency because inconsistency risks legal and cultural fallout.

Sales pushes for momentum because hesitation costs opportunity.

Each stance makes sense within its own reality. Each produces a different definition of success. And those definitions aren't just technical, they're emotional. They tie directly to incentives, safety, and reputation.

So when leadership announces a push for "alignment," it sounds collaborative. In practice, it's a redistribution of risk and authority. Someone's definition will prevail. Someone else's will be displaced. One group gains insulation; another absorbs accountability.

People sense this immediately, even if no one says it aloud. That's why conversations about metrics feel tense, even when they appear purely technical. The numbers are not the real issue, the consequences are.

And here's the uncomfortable truth: introducing AI doesn't neutralize this dynamic. It amplifies it. Faster decisions mean faster shifts in power. Automation doesn't erase politics; it accelerates the pace at which those politics play out.

METRICS, STORYTELLING, AND DEFENSIVE NARRATIVES

Metrics have always been more than numbers, they are narratives.

Organizations often say they want metrics for insight, but what they truly seek is reassurance or explanation: Are we succeeding? Are we at risk? Who needs to act? Who will be held accountable?

Metrics are inseparable from perception and the management of uncertainty.

Before AI, reshaping these narratives required effort. Reports had to be rebuilt, charts redesigned, and talking points rehearsed. That friction acted as a natural brake on how often stories could be reframed.

AI removes that brake.

It excels at summarizing, contextualizing, and filling gaps. It can explain variance with confidence and produce narratives that feel polished and authoritative. That makes it powerful, and dangerous in organizations that lack alignment on meaning.

When an answer feels uncomfortable, it's easy to ask again. Adjust the framing. Shift the context. Highlight different variables. Exclude others.

AI will oblige, not because it intends to mislead, but because it is designed to be adaptive and agreeable. This creates a new form of influence: the ability to iterate narratives without altering the underlying data. Whoever understands how to steer context can reshape the story repeatedly.

AI does not question whether a metric should exist. It focuses on how to explain it.

That distinction matters because it enables metrics everyone knows are incomplete to appear legitimate. AI accelerates storytelling, but it does nothing to resolve the deeper disagreements about meaning.

THE EMOTIONAL STAKES BEHIND "SOURCE OF TRUTH"

Few phrases spark more quiet tension inside organizations than "source of truth."

Technically, the idea seems simple: it's the system where data originates, the authoritative record, the canonical dataset. Clear enough on paper.

But in practice, that definition rarely satisfies. For most business users, truth is not about lineage; it's about utility. The "real" source of truth is whatever answers the question they have right now. If the official system doesn't deliver, they improvise. They export data, merge sources, build spreadsheets, and create their own calculations, not to defy governance, but to keep work moving.

From IT's vantage point, this looks like fragmentation. From the business side, it feels like survival.

AI magnifies this tension. By collapsing the gap between question and answer, it creates an expectation that the system knows everything, that it understands context and can provide a definitive response instantly. Few users pause to check lineage or provenance. They rarely distinguish between authoritative, derivative, or speculative sources. If the answer sounds credible and useful, it becomes truth by default.

That shift introduces real risk. Decisions, strategies, and actions increasingly rest on confidence rather than credibility. The danger isn't in the technology, it's in the assumption that speed equals certainty.

This is why alignment around "source of truth" cannot be solved by tooling alone. It's a trust problem, an education problem, and even then, it remains imperfect. People will always route around friction long before they escalate it. Systems may define authority, but human behavior defines reality.

WHY DEPARTMENTS DEFINE TERMS DIFFERENTLY

Every department lives in its own ecosystem, shaped by distinct pressures, timelines, and consequences. The risks differ, and so do the punishments. Finance fears being wrong. Operations fears being slow. HR fears inconsistency. Sales fears hesitation. IT fears instability. These fears govern behavior far more effectively than any written policy.

Definitions grow out of these realities. They are not arbitrary; they are adaptive responses to what hurts most when failure occurs. That is why reporting conflicts rarely hinge on accuracy. They hinge on perspective.

Two reports can both be correct and still contradict each other because they serve different purposes. One safeguards credibility. Another justifies investment. A third signals urgency. A fourth manages risk. Each reflects the lens of its creator.

When leadership encounters conflicting numbers, the reflex is to impose alignment, choose one version, standardize, enforce. But alignment without shared meaning creates a hollow performance of compliance. Rules exist on paper, while interpretation quietly shifts in practice.

Authority erodes without fanfare. Governance falters, not because governance is irrelevant, but because it assumes consensus where none exists.

True governance is not about writing rules. It is about creating shared meaning. Until that work is done, every mandate will be fragile, and every metric will remain contested.

HOW REPORTING DISAGREEMENTS STEM FROM BEHAVIOR

Reporting is never neutral, it shapes behavior as much as it reflects it.

Reports exist to provide answers, but those answers are rarely pure data. They are molded by fear, accountability, and incentive. Behind every chart lurks a set of questions: Why did we miss the target? Who will take responsibility? How do we explain this to the board without triggering fallout?

Metrics do more than measure performance; they manage perception.

AI now accelerates this dynamic. It adds speed, fluency, and polish, producing explanations that sound complete and authoritative. That confidence often replaces scrutiny. The question shifts from “Is this accurate?” to “Can I defend this?”

AI didn't invent this behavior, it supercharges it. It enables narratives to form quickly, even when the underlying disagreements remain unresolved. And when someone disputes an AI-generated explanation, the conversation rarely stays about numbers. It touches on influence, accountability, and trust, areas where pushback can feel uncomfortable and costly.

WHY ALIGNMENT IS THE ONLY PATH TO AI READINESS

Most AI missteps don't start with faulty algorithms, they start with human dynamics. AI thrives on clarity: shared definitions, trust, and a common understanding of priorities. When those foundations are missing, automation doesn't fix the problem; it magnifies it. Misalignment becomes faster. Ambiguity gets baked into outputs. Consider culture as the amplifier. In a metric-obsessed environment, AI won't create better thinking, it will turbocharge shallow compliance. People will chase numbers instead of outcomes, and gaming the system will become more efficient, not more intelligent. In contrast, when meaning drives decisions, AI strengthens judgment. It becomes a partner in reasoning rather than a substitute for it. AI doesn't rewrite incentives. It reveals them, sometimes brutally, by making visible what the organization truly optimizes for.

DATA AS A REFLECTION OF COLLECTIVE INTERPRETATION

Data is not objective in the way organizations want to believe. It doesn't stand apart from human influence, it carries the imprint of choices made long before it enters a system. What gets measured, what gets ignored, how questions are framed, and which answers are filtered all shape the story data tells.

On its own, raw data is inert. Meaning emerges only when humans interpret it, layering context, judgment, and experience onto numbers. In that sense, people function like systems too. We process streams of input, sights, sounds, emotions, memories, and apply filters constantly. We decide what matters and what fades into the background.

Our technical systems replicate this behavior because they are built by us. They inherit our assumptions, our blind spots, and our priorities.

This is why AI cannot operate without human oversight. Not as a backup plan, but as a fundamental requirement. AI lacks lived experience. It does not carry the weight of consequences. It cannot grasp what it costs to be wrong.

People can. And that difference is not a limitation, it is the reason judgment still matters.

SEMANTIC BATTLES AS CULTURAL BATTLES

Every fight over definitions is really a fight over culture. When people argue about what a term means, they are not debating semantics, they are negotiating values, priorities, and identity. No amount of automation can erase that reality.

Culture cannot be installed like software. It is lived, shaped by daily choices, and influenced by what happens under pressure. It adapts quietly and erodes just as easily. Executive messaging may set intentions, but behavior determines outcomes.

AI will not create culture, yet it will inevitably become part of it. It will mirror your incentives, expose blind spots, and amplify the level of maturity already present. If the organization treats data as purely technical, it will keep fighting the wrong battles, swapping tools instead of addressing habits, chasing clarity that never arrives.

Definitions matter because they decide what counts as real. And inside any organization, reality begins with people, not platforms. Technology can scale meaning, but it cannot invent it.

Why We Don't See Our Own Behavior

BLINDNESS IS NOT IGNORANCE. IT IS ADAPTATION

People often cling to the comforting idea that failure announces itself loudly, that broken systems are obvious, that inefficiency screams for attention, that if work were collapsing, alarms would sound across the organization. It feels reassuring to believe that dysfunction is self-evident.

But reality rarely works that way.

Most dysfunction doesn't arrive with flashing lights or sirens. It doesn't feel catastrophic while it's unfolding. It feels ordinary. It feels like the daily grind, doing what you can with the time, tools, and energy you have. And when something feels ordinary long enough, it fades from view. It becomes part of the landscape.

This is the first hard truth leaders wrestle with: people don't ignore dysfunction, they adapt to it. And adaptation, repeated over time, becomes invisible.

Consider your commute. Do you recall every detail of the trip from your front door to your desk? The way you held your keys, the sequence of steps through the garage, the angle of your mirrors, the countless micro-decisions at every intersection? Probably not. Those actions matter, you couldn't arrive without them, but your brain doesn't catalog them because doing so would waste energy. Anything that works reliably gets pushed into the background.

Work functions the same way. Every day, employees execute hundreds, sometimes thousands, of behaviors without conscious thought: physical movements, mental sequencing, prioritization, avoidance, risk assessment, emotional regulation. None of it feels deliberate once it's ingrained.

That isn't a flaw in human design; it's the design itself. Blind spots aren't signs of incompetence, they're the byproduct of conditional learning. When a pattern keeps you employed, paid, and out of trouble, your brain stamps it as safe. And once something feels safe, scrutiny disappears.

Here's where leaders often misstep: they interpret blindness as negligence. They assume that if someone isn't following the "correct" process, it must mean they don't care or don't understand. In truth, most people are following the only version of the process that allows them to function within the constraints they face.

Blindness isn't laziness. It's psychological armor. It's how people protect themselves from cognitive overload in environments that demand constant adaptation.

COPING IS NOT A SIDE EFFECT. IT IS THE SYSTEM

Every organization publishes an official playbook for how work should flow. And yet, alongside that idealized version, there's the reality, the way work actually gets done. The space between those two worlds is filled with coping strategies.

These strategies aren't acts of defiance. They aren't sabotage. They're practical responses to friction, ambiguity, delays, and relentless pressure. When systems fail to meet people's needs, work doesn't stop. People adapt. They improvise.

They return to what feels dependable.

Take the inbox. It hasn't endured because it's flawless. It endures because it feels familiar, like home turf. Email offers a sense of control. People know its rules. They know how to create folders, flags, and filters. They know how to impose order when chaos threatens. In short, the mailbox feels personal.

That feeling of ownership is more powerful than most leaders realize. When a system feels like it belongs to you, experimentation feels safe. When a system feels imposed, opaque, or sluggish, people search for alternatives that restore autonomy.

That's why spreadsheets morph into CRMs.

That's why shared mailboxes evolve into case management tools.

That's why personal task lists quietly replace enterprise workflow engines.

None of this happens because employees want to undermine governance. It happens because they're trying to deliver on expectations with the resources they trust.

Here's the uncomfortable truth: every workaround is a solution to a problem the organization chose not to solve. These coping behaviors don't need approval. They grow organically. And once they work, even a little, they spread. Someone shares a template. Someone forwards a chain. Someone copies a file. Before long, the workaround isn't a workaround anymore. It's the norm.

And norms rarely get questioned.

This is how coping hardens into culture.

WHY DYSFUNCTION BECOMES INVISIBLE

The most dangerous phrase in any organization isn't "this is broken." It's "this works."

When someone says a process works, they rarely mean it's efficient or effective. What they usually mean is that it hasn't failed loudly enough to demand attention. That's survival, not success.

Every process has flaws. Pretending otherwise isn't optimism; it's self-defense. A better answer to the question "Does this work?" sounds like:

"It works most of the time, but there are places where it breaks down."

That kind of honesty invites curiosity and improvement.

"It works perfectly" shuts the conversation down.

Why do people defend processes so fiercely? Because processes become personal. If you helped design it, you're invested. If you've learned how to navigate it, you're attached. If your competence depends on mastering it, criticism feels like an attack. That's why confidence often masks dysfunction.

Teams amplify this by creating shared narratives. They reassure each other that everything is fine. They normalize inefficiency by calling it reality. Over time, what started as a temporary compromise hardens into an unquestioned assumption.

Silence makes this worse. Leaders send messages, hear nothing back, and assume alignment. But silence rarely means agreement. It might signal fear. It might signal avoidance. It might mean people are overwhelmed, or that the message was never even read. Silence does not equal understanding.

Yet uncertainty feels harder to manage than quiet. So leaders accept the quiet. And in doing so, they reinforce the very blindness they hope to avoid.

THE DISTANCE BETWEEN INTENTION AND BEHAVIOR

People often assume that intentions shape behavior, but in practice, behavior quietly reshapes intention far more than we like to admit. No one starts the day planning to cut corners or undermine a system. They start with simple goals: finish the work, meet the deadline, keep things moving. Risk isn't introduced deliberately, it slips in while trying to make things easier.

The shift happens gradually. It doesn't feel like a slide into inefficiency; it feels like progress. Each adjustment seems reasonable. A workaround solves a pressing issue. A shortcut saves time. Viewed alone, every choice feels justified. Together, they form a pattern no one intended.

That's how teams drift. Not through reckless decisions, but through a series of small, logical steps that accumulate unnoticed. By the time someone asks why the process looks nothing like the original design, the answer is buried under years of adaptation. And that question always comes too late, because the system didn't break overnight. It evolved, one compromise at a time.

IDENTITY IS THE FINAL LOCK

People cling to what makes them feel capable. If your sense of worth at work comes from being quick to respond, you'll favor tools that keep you fast. If control defines you, predictability will feel like safety. And if expertise is your anchor, anything that exposes your judgment to challenge will feel like a threat.

That's why blind spots survive even when the evidence is clear. Seeing yourself honestly demands vulnerability, the willingness to admit that yesterday's strengths might be today's limitations. It's a costly move, psychologically and professionally, and most organizations don't reward it.

So people avoid it. They adjust. They rationalize. Eventually, the adaptation becomes invisible, and the original choice fades from memory. What began as a strategy for competence quietly hardens into a habit that shapes the future.

WHERE AI ENTERS THE PICTURE

AI never arrives in a vacuum. It steps into an ecosystem already shaped by human compromises, processes bent by survival tactics, cultures conditioned to avoid uncomfortable truths. It doesn't just join a workflow; it enters a story that has been unfolding for years.

This is why its presence feels unsettling in ways people struggle to explain. AI doesn't merely automate; it illuminates. It reveals patterns long ignored, reframes information we thought was settled, and exposes inconsistencies that teams have quietly learned to live with. When those blind spots surface, curiosity rarely comes first. Defense does.

That defense takes many forms. Sometimes it's outright dismissal. Sometimes it's endless re-prompting until the output feels safe. Sometimes it's leaning so heavily on AI that it becomes a crutch rather than a lens. In each case, the technology becomes another coping mechanism, another layer of adaptation rather than transformation.

Leaders use it to accelerate. Teams use it to sidestep hard conversations. Organizations use it as a badge of modernity while leaving old habits untouched. And in doing so, they risk amplifying the very dysfunction they hoped to escape.

AI will not fix what people refuse to face. If it's dropped into blind systems without reflection, it will magnify the drift, not reverse it. The danger isn't in the algorithm, it's in our predictability. Without deliberate introspection, AI doesn't change the game; it speeds up the same play.

DRIFT IS NOT FAILURE. IT IS MOMENTUM WITHOUT AWARENESS.

Organizations rarely implode overnight. They erode, slowly, almost imperceptibly. Drift doesn't announce itself with alarms; it feels like progress while it's happening. Each adjustment seems practical, even clever. And because the change is incremental, no one stops to ask where it's leading. By the time the consequences appear, the behaviors that caused them are no longer questioned, they're defended as best practice.

This is where many leaders misread the situation. When results decline, the instinct is to diagnose execution: more training, sharper tools, tighter processes, stronger accountability. Those remedies can help, but they often miss the deeper truth. The organization hasn't failed at its plan, it has been following a path no one consciously chose.

Drift is the outcome of adaptation without reflection. Every workaround introduced to solve a short-term problem nudges the system away from its original intent. Each deviation feels harmless, even smart, until the stack of small changes hardens into structure. What began as flexibility becomes the new normal.

That's how teams slide into chaos: not through reckless decisions, but through a series of reasonable ones that accumulate quietly. Drift is rarely dramatic. It's the tide that moves the shoreline while everyone is busy building sandcastles.

THE ILLUSION OF CONTROL THROUGH ABSTRACTION

Leaders rarely witness drift firsthand because what reaches them is already filtered. They see dashboards, KPIs, project milestones, artifacts that summarize reality without fully capturing it. These reports aren't lies, but they are translations. They strip away the texture of work, the friction where truth usually hides.

Abstraction is inevitable. No leader can watch every decision unfold or sit inside every conversation. But abstraction has a price: it smooths out the edges, removes emotion, and turns lived experience into neat representations. When a leader asks, "Are we on track?" the question isn't about how the work actually happens, it's about whether progress looks acceptable. And teams learn to answer in ways that keep things moving.

This isn't deception; it's survival. People quickly understand what leaders need to hear and provide it. Over time, leaders become fluent in reading these abstractions, yet less fluent in sensing when those abstractions stop mapping to reality. That's where blind spots grow.

Leaders themselves aren't exempt from drift. They operate under pressure from every direction, juggling expectations, deliverables, and their own coping strategies. They rely on mental models, simplified pictures of how work gets done. Those models are usually "good enough." Until they aren't.

And that phrase, good enough, conceals a lot. It hides the small compromises that accumulate, the shortcuts that become norms, the quiet adaptations that reshape the system without anyone noticing. By the time the gap between representation and reality becomes visible, the organization has already moved far from its original intent.

Drift doesn't announce itself. It whispers through abstractions, and leaders, busy and well-intentioned, often mistake the whisper for stability. The question isn't whether leaders can eliminate abstraction, they can't. The question is whether they can create moments to pierce it, to see the texture again before "good enough" becomes a trap.

"DO WHATEVER YOU NEED TO DO" IS A CULTURAL SIGNAL

Few phrases carry as much weight in an organization, or as much hidden risk, as this one:

"Do whatever you need to do to get it done."

It sounds empowering. It often comes from a place of trust or urgency. Leaders use it to signal flexibility, not recklessness. But beneath the surface, it sends a different message: that results outrank process, that speed eclipses integrity, that the "how" matters less than the "what."

Repeated often enough, this mindset reshapes behavior. People stop asking, What's the right way? and start asking, What's the fastest way? They prioritize completion over compliance, friction reduction over reflection. This isn't laziness, it's logic under pressure. When the system rewards output above all else, adaptation becomes survival.

Even high-performing organizations aren't immune. Drift doesn't announce dysfunction; it signals momentum without guardrails. And here's the part leaders often miss: drift isn't something that happens "down there." It's frequently a direct response to expectations set at the top, sometimes explicitly, sometimes implied.

Culture grows from what leaders reward, what they overlook, and what they abstract away. Incentives become habits. Habits become norms. Norms become invisible. By the time anyone notices, the organization has quietly shifted from doing things right to getting things done at any cost.

The question isn't whether urgency is necessary, it often is. The question is whether leaders can create urgency without eroding the principles that keep the system healthy. Because once "whatever it takes" becomes the default, the cost isn't just procedural. It's cultural.

THE COST OF "GOOD ENOUGH" THINKING

Imperfection isn't the enemy. In fact, it's often practical. Not every inefficiency deserves attention, and not every process warrants optimization. Sometimes the cost of fixing something far exceeds the benefit. Accepting "good enough" can be wise, until it quietly turns into "this works."

That shift is where the risk lives. Once a process is labeled as working, scrutiny fades. Curiosity fades. Learning stalls. What was once provisional becomes permanent, and permanence breeds attachment.

Attachment isn't just procedural, it's emotional. Teams invest time, energy, and identity into the systems they use. Even flawed processes offer familiarity, and familiarity feels safe. Change, by contrast, introduces uncertainty. And uncertainty is expensive, not in dollars, but in trust.

People carry memories of bad change. They remember initiatives driven by metrics instead of understanding. They remember tools imposed by outsiders who didn't grasp the work. They remember budgets burned without results. Those scars harden resistance.

So when new change arrives, even good change, teams hesitate. They harmonize with the status quo. They protect what they know. They wait for proof, sometimes until the initiative collapses under its own weight.

From the outside, this looks like resistance. From the inside, it feels like caution. Both perspectives are true. And unless leaders understand that tension, they'll misread hesitation as defiance instead of self-preservation.

The question isn't whether imperfection is acceptable, it often is. The question is whether "acceptable for now" is allowed to masquerade as "effective forever." That's where drift begins.

LEADERS HAVE THE BIGGEST BLIND SPOTS

It's uncomfortable to admit, but essential: leaders often carry the largest blind spots in any organization. Not because they lack care or commitment, but because their vantage point shields them from the friction that defines daily work. Leadership is altitude, and altitude changes what you see.

From that height, work appears as dashboards, KPIs, and summaries. Pressure arrives as accountability. Success is measured in outcomes. What rarely reaches the top is the emotional weight of navigating broken systems, the frustration, the compromises, the coping behaviors that accumulate over time. That distance matters because decisions are made from signals, not texture.

Leaders are trained by their environment to move fast. Speed is rewarded. Hesitation is punished. Over time, this creates a bias toward closure over exploration, a preference for answers that feel definitive, even when reality is messy.

AI slides perfectly into this pattern. It offers instant responses, polished summaries, and confident language. It feels like clarity. It feels like progress. And sometimes, it is. But speed without depth isn't clarity, it's acceleration. And acceleration without reflection magnifies drift.

Under relentless time pressure, leaders are especially vulnerable to using AI as a coping mechanism. Instead of asking people, they ask the system. Instead of sitting with uncertainty, they generate certainty on demand. The risk isn't obvious because the output looks convincing. AI can create the illusion of knowledge without understanding, answers that sound right but lack grounding. And because leaders are judged on results, not reasoning, that illusion often goes unchallenged.

Until it fails. And when it does, the failure isn't just technical, it's cultural. It reveals how easily convenience can masquerade as competence, and how quickly trust in process erodes when speed becomes the ultimate metric.

WHEN AI ACCELERATES DRIFT

AI doesn't create drift, it accelerates it. When an organization already prizes speed over reflection, AI becomes a turbocharger. When leaders lean heavily on abstractions, AI adds another layer of distance. When teams avoid questioning their own habits, AI makes that avoidance easier and more comfortable.

This is why resistance to AI often feels hard to explain. People sense something is off, but struggle to name it. The discomfort isn't about the tool itself, it's about what the tool reveals. AI rearranges information, draws connections that were previously ignored, and exposes patterns without regard for politics or tradition. It doesn't know which blind spots are sacred, and that makes people uneasy.

Responses vary. Some dismiss the output outright. Others keep re-prompting until the answer feels familiar. Still others surrender judgment entirely, outsourcing thinking to the system. Each reaction feels rational in isolation, but together they form a pattern, a coping mechanism disguised as progress.

And like all coping mechanisms, it offers short-term relief while quietly compounding long-term risk.

DRIFT IS PREDICTABLE

None of this should surprise anyone who understands how people respond under pressure. Individuals adapt. Teams smooth over friction until it feels normal. Leaders simplify complexity into abstractions. Systems reward speed because speed looks like progress. Over time, these forces converge, and drift becomes inevitable.

The real danger isn't drift itself, it's the invisibility of drift until the cost is undeniable. By the time the consequences surface, the behaviors that caused them have hardened into culture.

AI doesn't rewrite this reality; it exposes it. And exposure is uncomfortable because it strips away plausible deniability. When patterns become visible, ignoring them is no longer ignorance, it's a choice.

This is where leadership must change. Not by piling on more tools or tightening compliance, but by creating space for reflection. Organizations need environments where behavior can be examined without fear, where curiosity is rewarded instead of punished, and where AI serves as a lens for awareness rather than a shortcut for avoidance.

Blind spots don't persist because people refuse to change; they persist because most organizations aren't built to make seeing safe. When observation feels like judgment, curiosity dies. If reflection carries a cost, people will avoid it. The challenge for leadership isn't adding more tools or enforcing compliance, it's creating conditions where awareness can thrive without fear. AI should serve as a partner in that process, not as an accelerant for avoidance. When technology amplifies clarity instead of comfort, it becomes a catalyst for progress rather than a mirror we turn away from.

SEEING REQUIRES SAFETY. AND SAFETY IS RARE.

If blind spots were only about awareness, fixing them would be simple: show the data, highlight the pattern, and expect behavior to shift. That's the logic behind most transformation efforts, and the reason so many fail. The barrier isn't knowledge; it's emotion.

People don't resist seeing because they lack ability. They resist because seeing has consequences. It threatens identity, disrupts routines, and injects uncertainty into systems already stretched thin. Awareness feels like risk, and risk triggers self-preservation.

This is the part leaders often misjudge. Organizations excel at demanding transparency but struggle to absorb what transparency uncovers. When noticing a problem signals blame, extra workload, loss of status, or exposure of past decisions, people do what humans have always done under threat: they narrow their focus, shield themselves, and adapt to survive.

Blind spots endure because they serve a purpose. They are not flaws in perception, they are coping strategies. They allow individuals and teams to function under pressure without constantly confronting the discomfort of change. Until leaders design environments where observation is safe and curiosity is rewarded, no amount of data will dissolve those blind spots. They are not cognitive gaps to close; they are emotional defenses to understand.

WHY REFLECTION IS SO RARE AT WORK

In our personal lives, reflection feels natural, even necessary. We question habits, examine patterns, and weigh choices about health, relationships, and meaning because the feedback loop is immediate. The consequences land directly on us, and that proximity makes introspection safe.

Work operates differently. In most organizations, reflection carries risk unless the culture explicitly protects it. Asking why things are done a certain way can sound like criticism. Highlighting inefficiency can be branded as negativity. Admitting uncertainty can be mistaken for incompetence. So people stay quiet. They execute. They adapt. They move forward without asking the questions that matter.

This is where AI introduces a paradox. On one hand, it promises space, time reclaimed, insights surfaced, information reframed. It can extend human capacity, offering breathing room in environments that rarely allow it. But if the organization doesn't value reflection, that space doesn't last. It gets filled instantly with more output: faster responses, more decisions, higher throughput. The oxygen AI creates is consumed by the same fire that was already burning.

Instead of enabling reflection, AI becomes another mechanism for avoidance, a tool that accelerates doing rather than deepening thinking. That is the paradox leaders must confront: technology can't create a reflective culture on its own. If speed remains the ultimate metric, every gain AI delivers will be converted into more motion, not more meaning.

The question isn't whether AI can save time. It can. The question is what the organization chooses to do with that time, because if the answer is "produce more," the space for reflection disappears before anyone notices it was there.

THE COMFORT OF NOT KNOWING EXACTLY WHY

One of the most overlooked psychological forces in organizations is the safety found in ambiguity, not uncertainty about results, but uncertainty about causes. When the reasons behind success or failure remain hazy, people have room to maneuver. Effort can be credited for wins, circumstances blamed for losses, and accountability stays comfortably diffuse.

Clarity changes that dynamic. It narrows the space for interpretation. When AI begins mapping patterns, surfacing correlations, and exposing inconsistencies, it ties behavior to outcomes with uncomfortable precision. Suddenly, the story feels less negotiable.

This is where resistance often emerges, not as outright rejection, but as subtle deflection. Questions shift. Prompts are tweaked. Data sources are scrutinized. Edge cases are emphasized. Another iteration is requested. Each move looks reasonable in isolation, even healthy as skepticism. But when skepticism becomes a shield for comfort rather than a pursuit of truth, it turns into avoidance.

The fear isn't about being wrong; it's about being visible. Ambiguity has long served as a buffer, a soft fog that protects identity and intention. AI clears that fog. And when the landscape sharpens into view, the discomfort isn't technical. It's human. Because clarity doesn't just reveal systems; it reveals us.

LEADERS AND THE BURDEN OF VISIBILITY

Leadership sits at the center of this tension. The role carries expectations that are relentless: provide answers, project confidence, and keep the organization moving, even when the picture is incomplete. These pressures don't just influence decisions; they shape habits.

Enter AI, and the dynamic shifts. For leaders, it feels like relief. Gaps close instantly. Language appears polished. Complexity compresses into something that looks like clarity. Under pressure, that promise is hard to resist.

But relief has a shadow. When leaders lean on AI outputs without anchoring them in lived context, the gap between representation and reality widens. Decisions accelerate while understanding thins. It's not a flaw in character, it's a structural trap.

The system rewards speed and punishes hesitation. Reflection takes time, and time feels expensive. AI offers velocity, and velocity feels responsible, until it isn't. Because speed without depth doesn't solve complexity; it amplifies it.

The leaders most vulnerable to this trap aren't the least capable. They're the ones carrying the heaviest load, managing layers of ambiguity with no space to pause. And here's the hard truth: AI won't create that space for them. If reflection isn't deliberately designed into leadership practice, technology will only tighten the cycle, more answers, less understanding, faster drift.

The question isn't whether leaders should use AI. It's whether they can use it without surrendering the very judgment their role depends on.

WHAT IT ACTUALLY TAKES TO SEE DRIFT EARLY

Organizations often ask how to spot drift before it becomes costly. The instinct is to look for metrics, dashboards, alerts, early warning systems. Those tools matter, but they rarely tell the full story. Drift begins as behavior long before it shows up in numbers. It starts in language, in habits, in the quiet signals of adaptation.

You can hear it in phrases that sound harmless:

"This is just how it is."

"We don't have time to fix that right now."

"That's not how the system is supposed to work, but it's how we use it."

"Everyone does it this way."

These aren't complaints; they're coping strategies. Each one reflects a choice to normalize friction rather than challenge it.

Detecting drift early requires a different kind of listening. Not for failure, but for resignation. Not for breakdowns, but for patterns that feel inevitable. It also requires asking questions that open space for honesty without demanding immediate solutions:

"What makes this hard?"

"Where do you have to improvise?"

"What part of this process do you not trust?"

"What do you do when the system doesn't help?"

These questions sound simple, but they carry weight. They invite answers that resist abstraction, answers that expose the texture leaders rarely see. And that's why they're risky. Most organizations don't ask them often. When they do, they're not always prepared for what they hear.

Drift hides in plain sight. It speaks softly through adaptation, and the only way to catch it early is to listen for what sounds normal, because normalization is where drift begins.

THE DIFFERENCE BETWEEN HEALTHY STABILITY AND DANGEROUS STAGNATION

Resistance isn't always a problem, and stability isn't always denial. Some processes deserve to stay intact. Some systems deliver enough value to justify leaving them alone. Sometimes the disruption of improvement outweighs the benefit. Stability, in itself, is not the enemy, certainty is.

When teams can't explain where a process fails, that's not stability; it's blindness. When leaders can't describe how work actually happens, that's not alignment; it's abstraction. Healthy organizations hold two truths at once: "This works well enough for now" and "We know where it doesn't." That second truth matters most. It keeps curiosity alive, preserves flexibility, and allows learning to continue without forcing constant change.

AI can help sustain this balance, but only if it's framed correctly. Not as an unquestioned authority. Not as a substitute for human judgment. Its role is to act as a lens, sharpening what's already there, revealing patterns without dictating decisions. When AI becomes a tool for clarity rather than control, it strengthens reflection instead of accelerating drift.

AI AS A PARTICIPANT, NOT A SOLUTION

AI never enters the room as a blank slate. It carries the imprint of its training data, the constraints of its context, and the assumptions embedded in the questions we ask. It doesn't weigh consequences or feel the weight of risk. It doesn't shoulder accountability. It operates inside the same behavioral system as everyone else, not above it.

When organizations elevate AI to the status of an oracle, judgment gets outsourced. When they frame it as a lens for awareness, judgment is strengthened. That distinction isn't technical, it's cultural.

In cultures where reflection feels unsafe, AI becomes another coping mechanism, a way to move faster without looking deeper. In cultures where reflection is protected, AI acts as a mirror. And mirrors are rarely comfortable. They reveal patterns people would rather ignore, challenge narratives teams have invested in, and make avoidance harder.

That discomfort isn't a flaw. It's the function. The value of AI isn't in making us feel certain, it's in making us see what certainty has been hiding.

WHY BLIND SPOTS ARE THE ROOT OF AI RESISTANCE

AI resistance is often explained as fear of job loss, lack of technical skill, or generational gaps. Those factors exist, but they're not the core issue. The deeper resistance comes from exposure.

AI doesn't just automate tasks, it makes patterns visible. It strips away the cover of habit, ambiguity, and informal workarounds that people have relied on for years. Behaviors that once lived in the shadows become legible, and that visibility feels risky when safety isn't guaranteed.

People aren't resisting because AI is unfamiliar. They're resisting because it forces the familiar into the open. And when transparency arrives without protection, it feels less like progress and more like vulnerability.

This is why initiatives that focus only on productivity, efficiency, and automation often fail. They treat resistance as a technical gap rather than an emotional reality. They overlook the coping strategies that keep systems functioning. They attempt to optimize a system without first understanding the drift that has already reshaped its culture, turning what looks like progress into another layer of fragility.

THE LEADERSHIP SHIFT THAT MATTERS

The future of leadership in an AI-driven world won't be defined by who adopts technology first. It will be defined by who creates cultures where visibility feels safe, where noticing patterns isn't punished, where naming workarounds isn't seen as defiance, and where admitting uncertainty doesn't cost credibility.

Safety doesn't mean removing pressure. Pressure is part of work. What matters is acknowledging it and understanding how expectations, spoken or implied, shape behavior. People adapt to what leaders reward. If speed is the only metric, reflection disappears. If output is the only signal, honesty becomes expensive.

Leaders don't need to see every detail, but they do need to care about how seeing happens. That means designing systems that make reflection possible, not just execution. It means valuing candor as much as performance. And it means treating AI as a participant in human dynamics, not a cure for them.

Because AI won't rescue organizations from their own habits. It will reveal them. It will surface the patterns already in play, the assumptions already embedded, and the blind spots already normalized. The question isn't whether AI will show us who we are, it's whether leaders will create the conditions to face that truth without fear.

CHAPTER 7

The Real Cost of Chaos

THE QUIET CHAOS NO ONE BUDGETS FOR

Most leaders think they know what chaos looks like. They imagine the obvious kind, the kind that screams for attention: a system outage, a blown deadline, a project collapsing so dramatically it demands an emergency meeting and a postmortem. That's the chaos you can measure, the chaos that shows up in reports.

But the chaos that truly erodes organizations rarely makes noise. It's subtle, persistent, and almost polite. It hides behind good intentions and reasonable explanations. It wears the mask of progress, meetings that feel productive, timelines that sound rational, updates that reassure without delivering. It doesn't announce failure; it disguises itself as motion. As complexity. As "we're working through it."

Every organization carries this silent weight. Size doesn't matter. Funding doesn't matter. Maturity doesn't matter. The real question isn't whether it exists, it's how deeply it has been absorbed into the culture and how long it has been allowed to live unchecked.

Quiet chaos thrives in the gaps between perception and reality. When people assume alignment but operate on different maps. When leaders believe decisions are happening, yet nothing moves forward. When accountability is written down but never enforced. When collaboration becomes a ritual instead of a result.

This is the chaos that corrodes trust and drains momentum, not with explosions, but with slow leaks. And because it feels normal, it's the hardest to see and the easiest to excuse.

This isn't dysfunction in the dramatic sense, the kind that announces itself with chaos and collapse. It's subtler than that. It feels almost rational when you're inside it. People still show up. Meetings still occur. Emails still circulate. Work still gets done. On the surface, everything appears functional. But beneath that surface, progress stalls. Nothing moves forward in a way that truly matters.

Teams limp along, not because they're incapable, but because momentum never materializes. Decisions hover in limbo. Risk-taking evaporates. And since no single moment feels catastrophic, the organization convinces itself that this is normal, that this is simply how work works.

It isn't.

This is waste, but not the obvious kind. It's invisible because the effort isn't malicious or incompetent. It's fragmented, defensive, and misaligned. People spend more energy shielding themselves from uncertainty than pushing the organization toward clarity. Hours vanish in meetings designed to prepare for other meetings that never produce outcomes. Teams chase clarity that never fully arrives. They perform diligence without direction. They fill the calendar with activity because activity feels safer than commitment.

What makes this form of chaos so insidious is that none of these behaviors are inherently wrong. Collaboration matters. Risk mitigation matters. Consensus matters. Communication matters. But when these practices become substitutes for accountability instead of supports for it, they metastasize. They stop being tools and start becoming shields.

When responsibility is theoretical rather than practical, no one truly owns the outcome. When decisions are deferred under the banner of caution, the cost doesn't disappear, it compounds. It simply shifts downstream to those with the least authority to resolve it. Quiet chaos thrives in the space between responsibility and power.

People sense something is off, but they can't name it cleanly. They feel friction without permission to address it. They notice misalignment but lack the authority to fix it. So they adapt. They improvise. They create workarounds. They protect themselves. And while improvisation can feel heroic in the short term, it becomes extraordinarily expensive at scale.

This is where leaders underestimate the cost. They hunt for waste in budgets, headcount, tooling, and process diagrams. They rarely look for waste in hesitation, silence, and ambiguity. They don't measure the energy consumed by people trying to interpret what decisions mean for them personally. That work doesn't appear on dashboards. It lives in people's heads, in Slack threads that go quiet, in emails that never get answered, in decisions that stall because no one wants to be the person who gets it wrong.

This is why organizations can spend millions modernizing systems and still feel stuck. The system changes. The behavior does not. Chaos compounds because behavior compounds. Misalignment at the top multiplies as it moves downward. When leaders avoid decisions, teams learn to hedge. When priorities shift without explanation, people stop investing emotionally in outcomes. When clarity is inconsistent, trust erodes.

And trust doesn't fail loudly. It withdraws. People still do their jobs. They still attend meetings. They still respond when necessary. But they stop offering discretionary effort. They stop pushing ideas forward. They stop taking creative risks. They stop caring in the way that drives progress.

This is where inefficiency becomes truly expensive, not because people are idle, but because they are exhausted. Not because work isn't happening, but because it's happening without direction. Not because processes are broken, but because people no longer believe those processes will protect them. There's a cognitive tax in this environment that most organizations never account for.

When expectations are unclear, people spend mental energy just trying to understand what's expected of them. They question whether their work matters. They wonder if they're focused on the right thing. They second-guess decisions. They replay conversations. They wait for confirmation that never arrives. People have a fundamental need to feel successful, to believe their effort leads somewhere. When that feedback loop breaks, stress fills the gap. Frustration turns into irritability. Irritability turns into disengagement. Disengagement turns into attrition.

This is one of the biggest reasons people leave jobs. Not because the work is hard. Not because the organization is imperfect. People expect friction. They expect some chaos. What they don't tolerate is persistent ambiguity with no path forward. They don't stay in environments where success feels undefinable, where goals shift without explanation, and where expectations wobble like loose scaffolding.

Misalignment creates a trust deficit. People begin to question leadership. They question decisions. They question teammates. Eventually, they question themselves. And when trust erodes, people retreat to psychological safety nets. They fall back on behaviors that feel familiar and safe. They do what has protected them before.

This is where creativity dies. Critical thinking requires space. Innovation requires confidence. Both require a sense that effort will be recognized and risk won't be punished arbitrarily. Quiet chaos destroys that environment. People stop experimenting. They stop thinking expansively. They do exactly what's asked, nothing more. They comply instead of contribute.

From the outside, this looks like resistance. Leaders often misread this withdrawal. They assume people are lazy, change-averse, or unmotivated. In reality, people are conserving energy. They're protecting themselves from unpredictability. This isn't a character flaw. It's a rational response to an unstable system.

Culture begins to decay here, not the glossy version leaders talk about, but the real culture that lives inside teams. The microcultures where work actually gets done. These are the backbones of organizations. When they're healthy, they compensate for systemic imperfections. When they're damaged, everything becomes brittle.

This is why change efforts fail even when they're well designed. Change management professionals understand this intuitively. They focus less on tools and more on how people feel inside the change. Because culture isn't what leaders say, it's what people do when clarity is missing.

And this is where AI enters the story. AI doesn't arrive in a vacuum. It enters the behavioral ecosystem that already exists. It doesn't fix misalignment; it reflects it. It doesn't resolve indecision; it exposes it. If people are unclear, AI won't magically make them aligned. If leaders avoid accountability, AI won't create courage. It will either be used as a clarity tool or as a shield. And too often, it becomes the latter.

Leaders who don't trust themselves to make decisions increasingly outsource judgment to AI. They ask it questions not to inform conversation, but to bypass it. They treat it like a subject matter expert in a box. This feels efficient. It feels modern. It feels decisive. It is none of those things.

AI is powerful at surfacing patterns, revealing insights, and mapping trade-offs. What it cannot do is carry the weight of consequences. It cannot sense how a decision ripples through people, culture, and trust. That responsibility remains human.

When leaders lean on AI as an escape from hard conversations instead of a catalyst for them, they don't eliminate chaos, they amplify it. And the organization feels the shock almost immediately.

Chaos doesn't stay contained. It spreads like dye in water, tinting every interaction. Every input passes through the current state and emerges altered. If that state is chaotic, even the best ideas come out distorted.

This is why activity does not equal progress. Motion does not guarantee momentum. Chaos is not energy, it's noise.

Think of science: progress happens under controlled conditions. Variables are introduced deliberately. Outcomes are observed. Adjustments follow. Organizations thrive under similar principles. They need predictable rhythms to create psychological safety. They need consistency to free cognitive bandwidth. They need chaos in measured doses, not turbulence without boundaries.

Controlled chaos sparks innovation. Uncontrolled chaos forces survival. Most organizations blur the line. They mistake urgency for creativity. They confuse disruption with growth. They assume constant change sharpens people. In reality, it drains them.

And exhaustion carries a price tag. It appears later as missed opportunities, attrition, stalled projects, and wasted investments. It surfaces when AI initiatives promise transformation but deliver confusion. It shows up when leaders wonder why nothing sticks.

The true cost of chaos rarely appears on a balance sheet. It hides in what never happened, ideas abandoned quietly, talent that slipped away, momentum that never formed. And once chaos embeds itself, it doesn't fade. It multiplies.

THE FINANCIAL GRAVITY OF INDECISION

One of the simplest ways to detect chaos is to compare what an organization claims to value with what it actually enforces. Most companies have no shortage of documentation, policies, governance decks, rollout plans, operating models, playbooks, frameworks. On paper, everything looks deliberate and well-structured.

Then reality arrives.

Day one exposes the gap. In a chaotic environment, plans rarely survive first contact. Not because people are defiant, but because the plan collides with complexity. Ambiguity creeps in immediately. Questions surface that no one anticipated. Edge cases appear. Ownership blurs. Silence follows. And from that moment, cost begins to accumulate, quietly, relentlessly.

This is the part leaders rarely budget for.

There's a persistent illusion that clarity on paper guarantees compliance. That one round of communication equals alignment. That deviation is an anomaly rather than the norm. In truth, behavioral alignment is never perfect. If you're intentional and fortunate, you might reach 80 percent. The remaining 20 percent isn't noise, it's where most of the hidden cost lives.

Because people will always improvise.

They improvise when instructions don't fit their reality. When processes slow them down. When approvals stall. When answers never arrive. Improvisation fragments behavior, and fragmented behavior drives up operating costs. Every workaround introduces variance. Variance leads to rework. Rework creates delay. Delay translates into financial impact, whether through wasted labor, missed revenue, compliance exposure, or poor decisions made under pressure.

This isn't hypothetical. It's structural.

Roll out a new system. Deploy AI. Launch a new process. If behavior isn't accounted for, people will route around it. They'll fall back on what feels safe, spreadsheets, shared mailboxes, file shares, side conversations, shadow systems. Organizations spend millions on enterprise platforms only to watch the real work continue in informal tools because those tools feel dependable in chaotic environments.

Not because people dislike systems, but because systems assume clarity, and chaos erodes clarity.

The financial impact isn't limited to licensing waste. It shows up as duplicated effort, parallel processes, inconsistent data, conflicting reports, and meetings spent reconciling numbers instead of making decisions.

And then there's silence.

Silence is one of the most underestimated cost drivers in modern organizations. When communication stalls, work doesn't stop. People still make decisions, but with partial information. Or they wait. Or they escalate sideways. Or they hedge. Every unanswered message carries a cost. Every delayed response forces someone to context-switch, re-evaluate, or make assumptions. In remote and hybrid environments, this effect multiplies quickly.

Silence creates latency. Latency creates friction. Friction creates expense.

Leaders often rationalize silence as thoughtfulness, busyness, or risk management. But from the other side, silence feels like abandonment. And perception matters. Because when people can't tell whether silence means "no," "not yet," or "not my problem," they adapt. They make local decisions that feel safe. They defer big ones. They over-document. They over-communicate defensively. All of that costs money.

What's different now is that silence is no longer invisible.

AI has quietly rewritten the rules of organizational behavior. Work patterns, once invisible, are now measurable. Response times, engagement frequency, topic bias, avoidance, inconsistency: all of these can be inferred from data. It's no longer hypothetical. A report can now show that a leader answers only five percent of messages, and only on certain topics. That pattern exists whether anyone wants to acknowledge it or not.

Interpretation matters, of course. But the mere existence of this data shifts power dynamics. Avoidance is no longer a suspicion; it can be surfaced. And that visibility introduces a new category of risk, financial and reputational. Not because leaders are malicious, but because behavior leaves a trail. When organizations apply AI to their own communication and collaboration data, they uncover truths that were previously hidden.

This is where chaos becomes dangerous.

Indecisive leaders who lean on AI as a shortcut rather than a tool create a false sense of certainty. They believe they are acting decisively, when in reality they are outsourcing accountability. Asking AI for insight is not the issue. The issue is treating its output as a decision.

AI does not know your organization. It cannot grasp the political undercurrents, cultural sensitivities, or the emotional weight of past choices. It has no memory of consequences. When leaders bypass the human work of gathering the right voices, AI accelerates the wrong outcomes.

And financially, this is where things unravel.

One person, armed with AI-generated confidence, can make a decision that cascades into disaster, a mispriced investment, a compliance failure, a strategic bet built on incomplete context. The cost of that decision doesn't sit neatly in a single line item. It ripples. It appears in misaligned reporting, wasted analysis, reforecasting exercises, endless "explain-away" meetings, lost customer trust, and corrective projects that cost more than doing it right the first time.

Chaos in definitions compounds the problem. If teams don't agree on what metrics mean, AI won't resolve that ambiguity, it will amplify it. Different inputs produce different outputs, all stamped with the illusion of authority. Leadership then spends precious time adjudicating numbers instead of making decisions. The organization becomes obsessed with reconciling reality rather than shaping it.

This is where inefficiency turns existential.

Because the organization isn't just wasting money, it's misallocating attention. And attention is the scarcest resource leaders have. Chaos consumes it relentlessly. Every hour spent clarifying what should already be clear is an hour not spent innovating. Every meeting devoted to resolving misalignment is a meeting not spent moving forward.

Opportunity cost is the hardest cost to measure, and the most damaging to ignore.

When chaos dominates, innovation becomes theater. Teams chase initiatives that look impressive rather than those that matter. AI pilots multiply without coherence. Budgets scatter to appease politics instead of concentrating on impact. And when those initiatives fail, AI takes the blame.

That's the most frustrating part.

AI isn't failing because the technology is immature. It's failing because it's deployed into environments that haven't done the behavioral work required to support it. Organizations call this governance, adoption, or change management. Those labels miss the point. This is about understanding how your organization behaves under pressure, how decisions really get made, where fear lives, where power hides informally, where trust is fragile.

If you don't understand that, no amount of tooling will save you.

Financially, chaos shows up as drag, as leakage, as drift. As decisions that cost more to reverse than they would have to make thoughtfully. And because it accumulates incrementally, leaders underestimate it until the damage is irreversible. By the time it appears clearly on a balance sheet, the root causes are buried deep in behaviors normalized for years.

That is why chaos multiplies.

It feeds on avoidance. It thrives in silence. It grows when no one wants to be the person who slows things down long enough to think. The real competitive advantage may come from what feels counterintuitive: stopping long enough to make clarity possible.

WHEN CHAOS TURNS POLITICAL AND BREAKS TRUST

Chaos does not stay neutral for long.

When clarity is absent, politics fills the vacuum. Few truths make leaders more uncomfortable because they reveal incentives most would prefer to ignore. In uncertain environments, people rarely wait quietly for direction, they maneuver. They defend turf. They optimize for visibility and survival. AI has intensified this dynamic. Its high cost, ambiguity, and prominence make it a magnet for status, budget, and influence. Everyone wants proximity to the narrative of progress. Teams want to look innovative. Leaders want to be associated with transformation. Departments want ownership of the story. At first glance, this looks like enthusiasm. Beneath the surface, it often signals rivalry. AI initiatives are not always pursued for organizational benefit; many are driven by personal motives, recognition, relevance, security, career positioning. That doesn't make anyone a villain. It makes them human. But misaligned incentives turn innovation into a contest. Budgets become battlegrounds. Data becomes currency. Teams jockey for control, framing their approach as the "right" one while quietly undermining alternatives. This pattern shows up everywhere, between IT and business units, between centralized teams and embedded ones, anywhere authority is fuzzy and rewards are visible. The outcome is fragmentation. Instead of a unified strategy, organizations end up with competing pilots, duplicated investments, and fractured narratives. Progress stalls not because technology fails, but because trust erodes and collaboration collapses under the weight of politics.

Multiple initiatives sprout in parallel, each with its own interpretation of purpose. Definitions drift like loose threads. Architectures branch in incompatible directions. Data loses its integrity. And as trust thins, failure becomes a weapon. When projects stumble, blame turns into currency. Costs are inflated to kill rival efforts. Success stories are selectively framed to elevate status. Learning gives way to posturing.

This is the moment AI becomes politicized. It stops being a tool for progress and starts serving as ammunition in organizational turf wars.

What makes this dynamic even more dangerous is the illusion of certainty, the myth of expertise. In cultures that reward confidence, admitting uncertainty feels like weakness. So people posture. They speak in absolutes. They present fragments of understanding as if they were complete maps. This book exists because of that reality: nobody has a universal playbook. Not because AI is unknowable, but because every organization is its own ecosystem, with unique politics, behavioral norms, risk appetite, and a history of trust and betrayal.

Anyone promising a one-size-fits-all solution is selling a fantasy. Real progress demands collective wisdom, shared humility, and the courage to admit what we don't know. Yet chaos punishes humility. In volatile environments, uncertainty feels dangerous, so people double down. They push harder for control when collaboration is what's needed. They cling to their agenda instead of seeking alignment. And that is how trust fractures.

Once trust begins to crack, assumptions shift. People stop believing in positive intent. They start reading motives into every decision. A delay looks like sabotage. A question feels like a challenge. Communication turns defensive. And when trust disappears, everything slows. Standards lose meaning because teams no longer believe in them. Compliance becomes a performance. Reporting turns political. Even data becomes negotiable.

This is the point where employees burn out, not because the systems fail, but because relationships do. People can tolerate broken processes if they trust each other. They cannot endure broken trust.

The emotional toll is profound. Work feels draining, not because tasks are hard, but because the environment is unpredictable. Employees don't know which version of reality will apply tomorrow. They don't know which initiative will survive or which leader's priorities matter. So they stop investing emotionally. Creativity dries up. They stop challenging bad ideas. They stop offering alternatives. They do the minimum required, and nothing more.

Leaders often misread this withdrawal as resistance. It isn't. It's grief. Grief for the work that could have been. For the culture they believed in. For the promise of progress that never materialized.

This is why chaos is the enemy of AI readiness. AI thrives on consistency, shared definitions, stable processes, trust, and a willingness to surface truth instead of bury it. Chaos undermines all of that. When AI enters a disordered organization, it doesn't create clarity; it creates exposure. It reveals misalignment, avoidance, political games, decision paralysis. It shows who responds and who disappears. And when that exposure feels threatening, organizations often blame the technology instead of the behaviors it uncovers.

The organizations that succeed with AI aren't the ones with the most sophisticated models. They're the ones with disciplined behaviors. They understand that clarity isn't a gift, it's an act. Leadership means making decisions with incomplete information and owning the consequences. Collaboration isn't about shared meetings; it's about shared purpose. They accept that chaos can't be eradicated, only contained. So they build routines that create safety. They allow micro-innovation within those boundaries. They treat AI as a participant in the system, not as an overlord.

Most importantly, they invest in understanding how their organization truly operates, not how they wish it did. Because the real cost of chaos isn't just financial. It's momentum. It's trust. It's talent. It's the future opportunities an organization never explores because it's too busy managing friction.

Chaos multiplies when ignored. It shrinks when acknowledged. And leaders who learn to see it clearly gain something far more valuable than efficiency: they gain the ability to move forward with intention.

AI Enters The Relationship

WHEN A THIRD VOICE ENTERS THE ROOM

For most of modern work history, the relationship has been binary.

There has been the person and the work.

The employee and the task.

The leader and the decision.

The team and the process.

Everything else sat downstream from that relationship. Systems, tools, platforms, dashboards all shaped how work moved, but they were never part of the relationship itself. They mediated, constrained, accelerated, or obscured what people were doing, but they did not participate. They did not watch. They did not remember. They did not hold patterns up for anyone to see.

That is what has changed.

Not because this new presence understands work the way people do. Not because it grasps meaning, consequence, or context in any human sense. The shift is simpler and more unsettling than that. For the first time, something has entered the daily flow of work that can observe behavior continuously, connect fragments that usually remain separate, and do so without having anything to lose.

The relationship between people and work has not been replaced. It has been altered.

A third presence has joined it.

And any time AI enters a relationship, the dynamic shifts, even if AI never speaks. Even if it never decides. Even if it never asserts authority.

This is where most conversations about this moment miss the point. Leaders debate tools. Vendors highlight features. Analysts model efficiency. None of that captures what actually changes inside a living organization. The first shift is not speed or scale. It is exposure.

AI does not need approval.

It does not manage impressions.

It does not worry about blame or reputation.

It does not carry a personal story it needs to protect.

It simply registers what is there.

That does not make it wise. It does not make it neutral. It does not make it correct. It is shaped by what it has seen and limited by what it cannot understand. But it is unburdened by the social instincts that have always softened, filtered, or deferred what people see in one another.

What unsettles people is not accuracy. It is the absence of self-protection.

That absence reads as honesty. Not truth in any absolute sense. Not objectivity. But something closer to an unedited reflection of behavior over time.

And once that reflection exists inside the relationship, even silently, the relationship is no longer the same.

THE ILLUSION OF AN EGO-FREE VOICE

People often reach for words like neutral or objective when they describe AI. Those labels miss what is actually happening. The issue is not whether it carries human influence. The issue is that it carries no instinct to protect itself.

That absence changes everything.

Inside organizations, self-preservation rarely looks like ego in the obvious sense. It shows up as quiet shaping. It appears in how questions are posed, which details are emphasized, which exceptions are smoothed over, and which stories are delayed or left untold. Most of this happens before anyone sees an answer. It lives in framing, timing, and selection.

AI does not do that kind of shaping. It has nothing to defend.

It takes the question as it is. It works with what is put in front of it. It reflects patterns based on exposure, not on consequence. When it responds, it is not calculating how the response will land, who it might upset, or whether now is the right moment. It is not managing reputation or weighing personal risk.

It responds.

That is why people experience it as honest.

Not because it is more accurate. Not because it has special access to truth. But because there is no self-editing before the response appears. No softening. No strategic silence. No protective delay.

The problem begins when that feeling is mistaken for reliability.

What people are responding to is not truth, but emotional relief. The relief of being answered without friction. Of being met without judgment. Of not having to navigate the subtle resistance that so often accompanies human interaction at work.

This is especially potent under pressure. When uncertainty is high and time is short, responsiveness feels like competence. Consistency feels like fairness. A calm reply feels like authority.

Many people are not looking for the right answer in those moments. They are looking for something that will take their concern seriously, reflect it back in coherent language, and make them feel less alone in the decision. That response can feel grounding, even reassuring.

But responsiveness is not wisdom.

Being heard is not the same as being understood.

And agreement is not the same as being right.

Emotionally, those distinctions blur, particularly in environments that reward speed and discourage doubt. When comfort is mistaken for clarity, trust flows too easily. And that is where over-reliance begins, not because the response is flawless, but because it feels safe to accept.

AI AS THE FIRST NON-HUMAN OBSERVER

What changes when AI enters the relationship is not speed or reach. It is memory.

Organizations have always left behind a trail of behavior. Messages sent and not answered. Documents revised again and again. Approvals that linger. Decisions that circle without closing. Escalations that arrive late. Silence that stretches longer than anyone admits. None of this is new. It has always been there.

What kept it from mattering was not secrecy, but time. Evidence was scattered across moments, systems, and people. Holding it together required sustained attention and a willingness to remember longer than most organizations ever did. Context faded. Details dissolved. Each episode stood alone, easy to explain, easier to forget.

That protection is gone.

Remembering across time changes the rules. When yesterday does not fade and last quarter does not blur into anecdote, behavior stops resetting with each new conversation. Continuity forms, whether anyone asked for it or not.

This is where discomfort comes from. Not from being exposed as dishonest, but from being seen as consistent in ways no one intended to be. The distance between what is said in public and what happens in private no longer disappears on its own. The difference between careful language and reactive responses no longer lives in separate moments. Delays accumulate. Justifications stack. Patterns take shape.

These are not acts of deception. They are ordinary human adjustments. People shift tone depending on audience. They hedge when risk feels high. They soften when authority is near. They move differently in meetings than they do when the work actually lands. This flexibility is not a flaw. It is how people navigate complexity without breaking.

The problem is not that people adapt. It is that adaptation leaves a trace.

When memory holds those traces together, explanations lose their insulation. Each moment can still be justified on its own, but taken together they tell a story that does not disappear. No policy erases it. No permission is required. No governance framework can fully contain it.

Once continuity exists, it cannot be undone. It does not matter whether anyone meant for it to happen. Remembering changes what behavior means, because it removes the luxury of starting over every time.

WHY THIS FEELS THREATENING

The discomfort this moment creates has little to do with being watched and everything to do with stories colliding.

Organizations have always lived on narrative separation. Different audiences received different versions of reality, not always out of deception, but out of necessity. What leadership said publicly did not have to line up perfectly with how work actually unfolded. Formal updates could coexist with informal adjustments. Multiple accounts could all survive because they rarely met.

That separation was a source of stability. It allowed authority to function without constant challenge and identity to remain intact even when reality was messier than the story suggested.

What changes is not that every detail becomes known. It is that fragments begin to meet. When enough signals line up over time, they form a directionally consistent picture. That picture does not need to be complete to be disruptive. It only needs to be coherent enough to raise questions that no longer stay contained.

Once different people can look at the same traces and arrive at similar conclusions, narrative control weakens. Authority that depended on managing perspective starts to wobble. Not because someone has seized power, but because the story no longer belongs to a single voice.

This is where threat emerges.

It is not about loss of privacy or AI oversight. It is about losing the ability to keep accounts separate. When the polished version and the lived version are forced into the same frame, explanations collide. Gaps become visible. Tension surfaces between who someone believes themselves to be and what their actions repeatedly suggest.

That collision destabilizes more than decision-making. It destabilizes identity. Roles that were sustained by selective visibility begin to feel exposed. Confidence rooted in narrative authority gives way to uncertainty.

This is why reactions often target the implication rather than the substance. The issue is rarely the question itself. It is what the question threatens to collapse.

Interrogation is still necessary. Context still matters. Judgment still belongs to people, not systems. But once coherence appears, it creates an obligation to respond. A visible pattern cannot be dismissed simply because it is uncomfortable to confront.

THE MYTH OF OBJECTIVITY AND THE REALITY OF BACKGROUND

The most important shift here is understanding AI as a reflector of language, not a holder of truth.

What it produces is shaped by what it has absorbed. The words it chooses, the confidence of its tone, the structure of its answers all arise from patterns in how questions are framed and how information is presented. It does not arrive blank. It arrives preloaded with assumptions embedded in language itself.

That is what makes it persuasive.

Fluency carries authority. When something speaks clearly and coherently, it feels considered. When it responds without hesitation, it feels certain. But that certainty does not come from judgment. It comes from continuity. From repeating familiar structures back to us with polish.

This is where the risk lives. Hidden premises move faster when they are expressed fluently. Framing choices disappear behind smooth language. Assumptions sound like conclusions. Suggestions feel like findings.

The danger is not that the reflection is malicious. It is that it is convincing. When language flows cleanly, people stop examining what it rests on. They confuse coherence with correctness and articulation with insight.

Nothing about this relieves humans of responsibility. It intensifies it.

Once a fluent reflection enters the relationship, judgment can no longer be passive. Leaders are forced to ask not just whether an answer sounds right, but what it is quietly carrying forward. The framing matters. The question matters. The premises matter.

At that point, pretending the relationship is still a simple exchange no longer holds. When AI has entered, one that speaks well, remembers what it has been shown, and reflects assumptions back with enough clarity to make them hard to ignore.

WHEN PROCESS STARTS TELLING THE TRUTH

As AI settles into everyday work, it stops feeling theoretical. It shows up in the places organizations have long treated as settled ground: workflows, approvals, handoffs, metrics. Areas assumed to be stable because they are documented.

That assumption rests on a misunderstanding of what process actually is.

Process is not a neutral mechanism. It is behavior that has been repeated often enough to harden into form. What looks like structure is really habit made durable, shaped by pressure, incentives, and the need to keep things moving.

Because of that, process carries traces of how people actually navigate work. Not just what was supposed to happen, but what routinely does. Where things slow down. Where they stall. Where they get rerouted. Where responsibility quietly shifts.

Most organizations focus on the visible outcome. Did it complete. Did it meet the target. Did it clear the checkpoint. The movement in between is treated as noise.

When those in-between signals are held together over time, a different picture emerges. Delays repeat in the same places. Approvals linger with the same roles. Escalations follow familiar paths. Workarounds stop looking exceptional and start looking structural.

This is where exposure begins. Not by breaking process, but by revealing what process has been preserving. The documented flow still exists, but it no longer tells the whole story. A second account forms beneath it, built from lived behavior rather than design.

Once that gap becomes visible, it is hard to maintain the idea that process is simply technical. It is a record of how work actually gets done, and that record is far more revealing than any diagram ever intended to be.

WHY AI SEES WHAT HUMANS MISS

Humans are good at making sense of single moments. We struggle much more with continuity, especially when that continuity points back to people we rely on or systems we helped put in place. Forgetting is not a flaw. It is how work stays manageable. Each situation resets just enough for us to move on.

That is where the difference appears.

Once AI holds continuity across those moments, forgetting stops doing its usual work.

Nothing here comes from sharper thinking or deeper understanding. It comes from not letting go. When moments are held together instead of allowed to fade, patterns form without anyone having to decide to look for them.

Consider approvals, one of the most common failure points in any organization.

An approval waits.

Days pass.

Nothing happens.

On paper, this looks like a stalled step. In practice, it is usually treated as an isolated incident. The delay gets explained, the situation moves forward, and the memory clears. Next time, the same thing happens again, and it is explained again, as if it were new.

Most systems reinforce this cycle. They record status, not accumulation. They tell you something is late, not that it is always late in the same way, in the same place, for the same reasons.

When continuity is preserved, that insulation disappears.

The question stops being what is blocked and shifts to what keeps blocking it. Not once, but repeatedly. Not as a one-off, but as a pattern.

At that point, explanations multiply. The issue may be overload. It may be hesitation. It may be competing priorities. It may be unclear ownership. It may be incentives that quietly reward delay. None of these are surprising. What is different is that they stop being hypothetical.

Holding moments together does not produce answers. It produces plausibility. It narrows the field of excuses that can be reused indefinitely.

That alone is enough to unsettle people. Not because anything new has been revealed, but because forgetting is no longer doing its usual work.

WHEN INSIGHT TURNS UNCOMFORTABLE

Organizations are comfortable with insight as long as it points outward. The moment it turns back toward how work is actually done, the tone changes.

Blaming a system is familiar ground. Systems fail. Tools misfire. Processes break. Those explanations are safe because they keep responsibility abstract. What is harder to face is that many breakdowns are not mechanical at all. They are adaptive responses. Decisions are delayed because choosing creates exposure. Approvals are held because authority is one of the few protections people feel they still control. Work that does not map cleanly to evaluation quietly slides down the list, no matter how important it looks on a plan.

These patterns were always present. What changes is that, with AI holding continuity, they stop appearing as isolated incidents.

When traces accumulate, signals no longer arrive one at a time. They arrive together. A delay here might once have been easy to dismiss. A single workaround could be rationalized. A missed commitment could be explained away. But when the same shape appears again and again, it stops being noise.

This is the moment discomfort sets in.

The issue is not exposure for its own sake. It is the demand to interpret what is now visible. Patterns ask questions. They force a choice between understanding and avoidance. Once a sequence makes sense as a whole, denial becomes an active decision rather than a default state.

That is why reactions often turn defensive. Not because the picture is complete, and not because it is beyond dispute, but because it is coherent enough to implicate how people see themselves and how they justify their actions.

An uncomfortable pattern does not need to be proven beyond doubt to matter. It only needs to be clear enough that it can no longer be ignored.

THE COLLAPSE OF PLAUSIBLE DENIABILITY

Before this shift, fragmentation did important work. Separate systems, separate conversations, separate memories allowed each moment to stand on its own. Context expired. Evidence dispersed. Explanations remained local and temporary.

That insulation no longer holds.

Once fragments align, coherence forms. It does not arrive as a verdict. It arrives as a shape that can be recognized again. And once that shape exists, it cannot be unseen.

Access can be limited. Outputs can be restricted. Interfaces can be removed. None of that restores the earlier state. The knowledge that a pattern exists changes how everything that follows is interpreted. Each new signal is no longer neutral. It either fits or it does not.

This is why reversal is so difficult. Coherence does not depend on constant visibility. It depends on memory. Once people have seen how pieces connect, they carry that understanding with them. Even partial access is enough to keep the structure intact.

From that point on, explanations behave differently. They are no longer evaluated in isolation. They are weighed against what is already known to repeat. Justifications that once worked lose their effectiveness, not because they are false, but because they are incomplete.

This is where deniability truly ends. Not when information becomes available, but when coherence becomes durable. Once the story holds together, it does not dissolve simply because someone wishes it away.

THE ETHICAL EDGE OF VISIBILITY

This is the moment where a real choice appears.

Understanding how work unfolds is not the same as acting on that understanding. Once visibility exists, the temptation is to use it to correct behavior instead of to examine the system that produced it.

Seeing delays, inferring patterns, and connecting context can feel like permission to intervene. The move is subtle. Insight shifts from a tool for learning into a mechanism for enforcement, often without anyone naming the change.

People do not operate in straight lines. Judgment has rhythm. Focus comes in waves. Some work demands speed. Other work demands pause. Compressing that variability into constant scrutiny turns difference into defect.

Someone thinking deeply starts to look idle.

Someone weighing consequences starts to look slow.

A team working through uncertainty starts to look misaligned.

None of this comes from the visibility itself. It comes from how people choose to use it.

This is where restraint matters.

Using insight to understand systems strengthens an organization. Using it to police individuals weakens it. The first expands judgment. The second replaces it with control. One builds resilience over time. The other trades trust for short-term order.

Skilled people recognize the difference immediately. They know when insight is being used to improve the work and when it is being used to manage them. When the line is crossed, they stop offering their best thinking, or they leave.

Ethics, in this context, is not about rules or safeguards. It is about what leaders do after they see clearly, and whether they choose understanding over control.

WHY GOVERNANCE ALONE IS NOT ENOUGH

Many leaders believe this problem can be solved with policy.

It cannot.

Policies, standards, and committees create structure, but they do not make decisions. They produce artifacts. Those artifacts can guide action, but they cannot interpret behavior, and they cannot absorb consequence. Treating them as a substitute for judgment is where governance quietly breaks down.

Organizations already operate with an understanding that human behavior is imperfect. People misjudge situations. They respond emotionally. They bend systems to survive pressure designers never anticipated. This has always been true, and organizations tolerate it because the alternative is rigidity that stops work altogether.

What changes is not the presence of risk. It is the visibility of it.

When insight was difficult to obtain, discretion was built into the system by default. Gaps remained unseen. Ambiguity softened accountability. As visibility increases, that insulation disappears. Restraint no longer comes from scarcity. It has to come from choice.

This is where governance either matures or collapses.

No framework can decide whether a pattern signals a constraint or a failure. No rule can determine when hesitation reflects care versus avoidance. No automated check can distinguish between overload and negligence. Those judgments require context, proximity, and responsibility. They require leaders who are willing to stay engaged rather than delegating interpretation to process.

Behavior does not scale cleanly. Interpretation cannot be automated. The moment governance tries to replace involvement with documentation, it stops governing and starts deferring.

The real question is not whether oversight exists. It is whether anyone is willing to stand behind the decisions that follow visibility.

Seeing creates obligation. What happens next is not a technical matter. It is a leadership one.

WHY PROCESS WAS NEVER THE PROBLEM

The mistake was never the dashboards themselves. It was what organizations expected them to explain.

For decades, process was treated as the problem. When outcomes disappointed, the response was to redesign the flow, replace the tool, add another layer of reporting. Behavior was assumed to be noise, something to average out or correct later. That assumption let a great deal go uninterpreted.

Dashboards told clean stories. They summarized outcomes, smoothed friction, and compressed variability into something manageable. That made them useful, but it also made them misleading. Not because they were wrong, but because they stopped short of the question that actually mattered.

Why does the same step slow down every time?

Why do handoffs work in theory but fail in practice?

Why do exceptions become routine?

Those questions were always present. They were just expensive to answer, and easy to avoid.

This is where the excuse disappears.

Once behavior is visible alongside process, it becomes clear that diagrams were never wrong. They were incomplete. They captured intention, not adaptation. They showed design, not survival. And by focusing exclusively on flow, organizations avoided confronting how people actually navigated risk, pressure, and incentive inside that flow.

Modernization stalled because it targeted structure instead of behavior. New systems were layered on top of old patterns. Automation accelerated what already existed. Nothing fundamental changed.

What is different now is not capability. It is exposure.

When behavior can no longer be treated as incidental, blaming process stops working. The question shifts from what needs to be optimized to what has been tolerated for years without interpretation.

You cannot automate your way out of that. You can only stop pretending it was invisible.

THE RISK OF MISINTERPRETATION

This is the point where distinction matters.

What becomes visible at this stage is signal, not judgment. Patterns suggest direction. They do not deliver conclusions. Treating one as the other is where damage begins.

AI holding these patterns is not the one making the judgment.

Inference can tell you what tends to happen. It can surface repetition. It can narrow the field of explanations. What it cannot do is render a verdict about capability. That remains a human responsibility, rooted in context, history, and intuition earned over time.

Potential does not announce itself cleanly. Growth is uneven. Struggle and excellence often share the same early signals. Someone who falters under one set of conditions may thrive under another. Someone who hesitates today may lead tomorrow. These distinctions do not live in aggregates or likelihoods. They live in judgment.

Misuse starts when inference is treated as final.

When leaders act on patterns as if they are conclusions, trust erodes quickly. People stop stretching. They stop trying things that might fail. They stop telling the truth about what they do not yet know. The cost is not just morale. It is learning.

There is a quiet irony here. The more insight is used to close questions, the less insight remains available. Behavior shifts to self-protection. People optimize for what is measured. They avoid what feels risky. They comply instead of thinking.

This happens faster than ignorance ever did. Not because the signal was wrong, but because it was treated as an answer.

Once that line is crossed, visibility stops expanding understanding and starts narrowing it.

THE REAL SHIFT AI INTRODUCES

The real shift here is not automation. It is accountability for interpretation.

Once coherence exists, not seeing is no longer credible. Patterns do not have to be perfect to matter. When enough aligns to form a shape, ignoring it becomes a decision rather than an accident.

That is why AI changes the relationship. It does not force action, but it removes the shelter of unawareness. It makes silence legible.

What follows is not about capability or efficiency. It is about response. How leaders interpret what is now visible, and whether they engage with it honestly, says more about the organization than the patterns themselves.

WHEN IDENTITY STOPS BEING PERFORMATIVE

Most organizations rely on narrative long before they rely on structure.

People present themselves as capable.

Leaders present certainty.

Teams present unity.

This is not deceit. It is adaptation. Over time, people learn which signals protect them and which put them at risk. They shape their outward story to fit the environment they are in. That shaping becomes identity, reinforced through repetition.

The strain appears when behavior does not line up cleanly with that story.

Single moments are easy to explain. Context shifts. Pressure rises. Exceptions happen. Each instance can be justified on its own. What unsettles people is not any one contradiction, but the accumulation of them.

When actions repeat in ways that quietly diverge from the narrative, the story starts to thin. Patterns form that no longer match how individuals or teams understand themselves. The gap is not always large, but it is persistent.

This is where exposure becomes existential.

Identity depends on coherence. When accumulated behavior begins to tell a different story, the self can no longer be maintained through explanation alone. It is not that anyone is accused. It is that the narrative loses its authority.

What remains is a question that cannot be deferred: which version is real, the one that has been told, or the one that has been lived.

THE DIGITAL FOOTPRINT NOBODY MEANT TO LEAVE

Every role leaves traces behind. Not because anyone is being watched, but because work happens through communication. Messages sent in haste. Replies delayed. Decisions revisited. Approvals sped up or set aside. Documents revised again and again. Calendars filled, emptied, reshaped.

None of this is deliberate evidence gathering. It is simply the residue of doing the job.

On their own, these moments mean very little. Any single message can be explained. Any delay can be justified. Any decision can be contextualized. No individual action defines a person.

What changes is accumulation.

When ordinary communication adds up over time, it stops behaving like isolated noise. Tendencies emerge. Not because anyone intended them to, but because repetition has a way of settling into shape.

A leader who speaks about empowerment but repeatedly steps in to override decisions.

A manager who emphasizes urgency yet routinely responds late.

An executive who champions transparency but consistently avoids difficult exchanges.

Each instance makes sense on its own. Together, they form a pattern.

These patterns are not born of deception. They grow out of adaptation. Pressure, incentive, risk, and self-preservation all play a role. People do what works locally to get through the day, the week, the quarter. The story that forms is rarely planned.

What changes is not the content of any single interaction. It is the scale at which those interactions can now be held together. Once that happens, identity can no longer be sustained by role or intention alone.

There is no accusation here. There is only continuity. And once continuity exists, the distance between who someone believes themselves to be and how they consistently act becomes harder to ignore.

AUTHENTICITY IS NOT PERFECTION

Authenticity is often confused with flawlessness.

It is not about having the right answer every time. It is not about perfect consistency or complete transparency. People do not expect that, and they rarely demand it.

What people do need is coherence.

Visible inconsistency is survivable. Everyone adapts. Everyone adjusts. A misstep can be understood. A change of mind can be respected. Learning in public does not erode trust.

What corrodes trust is something else entirely. It is the presence of patterns that are never acknowledged. When behavior repeats in ways that contradict stated principles, and no explanation is offered, unpredictability sets in. Not the healthy kind that comes from complexity, but the kind that feels ungrounded.

Trust does not require agreement. It requires orientation. People want to know how decisions are being made and what logic is guiding them. Even an unpopular outcome can be accepted when the reasoning behind it is visible.

When accumulated behavior starts to tell a story that differs from the one being presented, the gap becomes difficult to ignore. The issue is not that someone fell short. It is that the pattern is allowed to persist without acknowledgment.

Once continuity makes those patterns visible, the pressure shifts. It is no longer about performing the right moments. It is about recognizing the shape that has formed over time.

Acknowledging that shape is what preserves trust. Pretending it does not exist is what breaks it.

WHY FEEDBACK HAS ALWAYS BEEN UNSAFE

Most people are not short on self-awareness because they refuse to learn. They are short on it because experience has taught them that honesty comes with consequences.

Pointing out inconsistency, confusion, avoidance, or misalignment has rarely been rewarded. In many organizations, it has been remembered. Power makes candor expensive. Over time, people learn what is safer to leave unsaid. Silence is not apathy. It is training.

This is how gaps persist. Leaders are not surrounded by deception. They are surrounded by adaptation. Others absorb the risk by withholding what they see.

What changes when visibility increases is not that new truths appear, but that old ones surface without asking permission. Patterns that were noticed privately begin to stand on their own. The risk shifts from speaking to responding.

That shift reopens a familiar fear. If patterns can be seen without someone volunteering them, how leaders react matters more than ever. Curiosity signals that understanding is welcome. Defensiveness confirms what people already learned long ago.

The danger is not exposure itself. It is the replay of old consequences under new conditions. When visible patterns are met with blame or denial, silence does not disappear. It hardens.

Nothing here is created by the technology. The response was already there. Visibility simply brings it back into play.

THE TWO-FACED MYTH

It is tempting to label inconsistency as duplicity. That shortcut misses what is actually happening.

Most people are not operating with two versions of the truth. They are responding to context. Behavior shifts with audience, medium, and perceived risk. Writing allows distance. Conversation invites immediacy. Formal exchanges reward caution. Informal ones reveal tone. These variations are not deceit. They are human.

The separation between an official account and a lived one has always relied on distance. Different settings allowed different versions of reality to coexist without colliding. What was said in one place did not have to fully align with what happened in another.

That separation is harder to maintain once continuity forms.

When behavior repeats across situations, it stops behaving like context and starts behaving like character. Not in a moral sense, but in a structural one. What looked like adaptation begins to read as pattern.

This is where the duality collapses. The formal story and the lived one no longer travel on separate tracks. They intersect often enough that the gap becomes visible.

The discomfort comes from predictability. Ambiguity once softened contradictions and preserved identity. When repetition removes that ambiguity, the shelter disappears.

What is left is not an accusation, but a question: which version carries more weight, the one that is presented, or the one that keeps showing up.

WHEN INFERENCE BECOMES ACCOUNTABILITY

What changes here is not the existence of inference, but its weight, and AI is what gives it that weight.

You no longer need a declaration to justify attention. When AI holds behavior together long enough for alignment to appear, questions become reasonable on their own. Explanation stops being optional once repetition is visible.

This is not a new standard. It is how serious inquiry has always worked. Patterns invite scrutiny. Consistency invites interpretation. What AI changes is how difficult it becomes to look away from that consistency.

When AI surfaces the same inference again and again, it creates obligation. Not to accept a conclusion, but to engage with what the pattern suggests. Dismissing the signal rarely reflects concern about how it was formed. More often, it reflects discomfort with what it implies.

At that point, intent becomes secondary. Whether the pattern was deliberate or accidental matters less than the fact that AI has made it legible. Once it is visible, choosing not to respond is still a response.

Choosing not to respond does not preserve neutrality. It becomes part of the pattern.

This is where responsibility shifts. Not because AI decides anything, but because interpretation is no longer confined to position. When AI makes inference durable, accountability follows, and that change does not reset.

THE HUMAN LINE AI CANNOT CROSS

There is a boundary here that does not move.

Judgment that carries consequence remains human. So does moral ownership. So does living with what follows.

AI can surface patterns, connect signals, and hold continuity over time. It cannot decide who someone is becoming, what they should be trusted with, or how responsibility should be assigned. Those calls do not live in systems. They live in experience, context, and the willingness to own outcomes.

People recognize this instinctively. It is why decisions that truly matter are still made face to face, even in environments saturated with information. Not because evidence is ignored, but because evidence alone is insufficient.

Insight can inform judgment. It cannot absorb its weight.

The moment consequence-bearing decisions are treated as outputs rather than choices, something essential is lost. Responsibility thins. Ownership blurs. Leaders retreat behind signals instead of standing behind decisions.

People do not resolve into patterns. They carry history, intention, and the capacity to change. AI can reveal what has been consistent. It cannot determine what should be.

Confusing those two is where ethical failure begins.

WHY HIDING IS NO LONGER A STRATEGY

The most unsettling shift is not that problems can be seen, but that hiding them no longer works.

For a long time, fragmentation offered cover. Information lived in different places. Context stayed local. Assembling a full picture required effort most people did not have. That friction acted as protection, not because anyone was being unethical, but because dispersion made scrutiny difficult.

That protection is gone.

Once coherence exists anywhere in the system, fragmentation stops doing its old job. You can restrict access. You can narrow visibility. You can slow circulation. What you cannot do is erase the fact that a story now holds together.

Inference does not require total access. It only requires enough alignment to recognize a shape. Once that happens, explanation changes. Each new signal is read in relation to what is already known.

This is why roles that once felt insulated now feel exposed. The same visibility that clarifies frontline constraints also reaches upward. Authority no longer guarantees separation. Identity no longer resets by position alone.

This is not a crisis. It is a test.

What matters now is coherence. Not perfection. Not uniformity. Coherence. And coherence has always been what trust rests on, whether organizations acknowledged it or not.

LEADING WHEN THE MIRROR IS ALWAYS ON

Once visibility becomes part of everyday work, the challenge shifts. The difficulty is no longer in seeing what is happening. It is in deciding how to respond to what is now visible.

For years, leadership operated with the benefit of distance. Insight took effort. Patterns surfaced slowly. That delay created room for discretion, interpretation, and, at times, deferral. Not because leaders were avoiding responsibility, but because the structure allowed it.

That buffer no longer holds.

When coherence forms quickly, hiding stops being a strategy. Not because it is wrong, but because it no longer protects anyone. What remains is response.

This is where leadership is redefined.

Leadership is no longer about managing what is seen. It is about resisting the urge to use visibility as leverage. It is about interpreting patterns without collapsing them into blame. It is about deciding when to act, when to wait, and when to acknowledge constraints without turning them into verdicts.

Restraint becomes the measure. Not silence, but control over how insight is applied. Interpretation replaces reaction. Ownership replaces deflection.

AI does not force these choices. It only removes the excuse not to make them. What leaders do next, and whether they stand behind the consequences, is what now defines leadership.

THE NEW RESPONSIBILITY OF INTERPRETATION

AI brings signals into view. Nothing more.

It shows where behavior gathers, where inconsistency repeats, where process buckles under human load, where stated intent no longer matches lived impact. That visibility is not a conclusion. It is an invitation to interpret.

What follows is not optional.

Once patterns are visible, choosing not to respond is still a decision. Waiting is a choice. Silence is a position. Deferral carries consequence just as action does. Leaders do not remain neutral by withholding judgment. They simply make it implicit.

This is where leadership is tested.

The failure is not lack of information or immature technology. The failure is treating visibility as if it absolves responsibility. Signals do not decide. People do. And the moment leaders allow inference to harden into verdict without ownership, trust erodes.

Leadership here is not about speed. It is not about proving control. It is about standing behind interpretation. Acting deliberately. Naming uncertainty. Owning the consequences of whatever choice follows.

Seeing changes the ground. From that point forward, not acting is still acting.

THE DIFFERENCE BETWEEN CLARITY AND CONTROL

AI forces clarity. It does not require control.

Clarity expands understanding. Enforcement narrows behavior. Confusing the two is how organizations lose judgment in the name of order.

When clarity is used well, it deepens insight into how work actually functions. It reveals where constraints stack up, where load concentrates, and where incentives quietly pull people in opposing directions. In those moments, clarity becomes a tool for redesign. Systems adapt. Expectations become more realistic. Decisions improve.

When clarity is used poorly, it becomes a mechanism for compression. Behavior is tightened. Variance is treated as error. People are pushed toward compliance rather than supported toward better judgment. What looks like discipline at first slowly drains discretion, creativity, and trust.

The distinction has nothing to do with tooling. It rests entirely on how leaders interpret what they now see.

Are people treated as thinking participants or as units to be corrected?

Are patterns read as signals to learn from or as justification to intervene?

Does insight widen the range of possible responses, or does it collapse them into a single acceptable path?

AI does not answer these questions. It amplifies them.

WHAT ETHICAL MATURITY ACTUALLY LOOKS LIKE

Ethical maturity, in this moment, is not about restricting tools or concealing information. It shows up in how leaders behave once insight is available.

The test arrives when patterns are visible and action would be easy. When pressure builds to correct, to discipline, to demonstrate control. Ethical maturity is the decision to pause there. To treat visibility as a reason to understand more deeply, not as permission to punish quickly.

This kind of leadership does not announce itself. It is visible in what leaders choose not to do. In their willingness to ask what conditions produced a pattern before deciding who is responsible. In their refusal to turn incomplete understanding into certainty just to satisfy demand for action.

Learning in those moments takes more effort than enforcement. It requires staying with ambiguity long enough for meaning to emerge. It requires resisting the instinct to optimize people the way systems are optimized, reducing complexity to something easier to manage.

Visibility changes the balance of power. Stories can be checked. Narratives can be compared. Authority no longer rests on what can be hidden or deferred. That makes restraint harder and more important.

When leaders respond to insight with curiosity instead of correction, they set a tone that travels. When they choose understanding over display, trust has room to grow. That is what ethical maturity looks like when insight is no longer scarce.

WHY AI CHANGES POWER WITHOUT CHOOSING SIDES

AI does not take sides. It does not align itself with employees or leaders, management or labor.

What it changes is who can make sense of what is happening.

The ability to examine patterns, test explanations, and connect evidence is no longer confined to role or rank. Access matters more than title. Interpretation is no longer the exclusive domain of those at the top.

This does not remove hierarchy. It alters what hierarchy has to stand on.

Position by itself carries less weight. Narrative by itself carries less protection. Explanations now have to hold together when viewed from more than one angle.

As a result, credibility shifts. It moves toward coherence. Leaders whose actions align over time find that trust accumulates more quickly. Leaders whose authority depends on performance without consistency find that gap noticed sooner.

Nothing here is punitive. There is no judgment being handed down. Patterns are simply available to more people, and availability changes how authority is experienced.

THE FINAL MISUNDERSTANDING

The last misunderstanding to clear away is the belief that something fundamentally new has arrived.

What has changed is not the nature of work or judgment. What has changed is that the gap between them no longer stays hidden. Choices that were once obscured by complexity now leave a trace. Avoidance, adaptation, and tolerance have always shaped outcomes. They were dispersed enough to avoid confrontation.

When difficult conversations are deferred, the deferral accumulates. When workarounds become routine, the routine takes shape. When dysfunction is endured, the endurance becomes visible. None of this is created. It is revealed.

That is why the shift feels unsettling. The familiar protections no longer hold. Complexity stops absorbing responsibility.

The value is not that something new is being imposed, but that what has always been present can no longer be dismissed as incidental.

THE FIRST HONEST PARTICIPANT

AI is not honest because it is correct. It is honest because it cannot look away.

It has no stake to defend and no identity to preserve. It does not manage impressions or weigh consequences. It simply holds what happens long enough for it to be seen.

That does not make it a judge. It does not confer authority. It does not make decisions. Meaning still comes from people, and responsibility still rests with them.

What changes is AI will not forget, will not soften, and will not turn aside when patterns form. AI does not accuse. It does not explain. It remains.

In that sense, AI becomes the first participant in work that forces humans to confront themselves.

Not as individuals. Not as villains or heroes. But as systems of behavior operating under pressure.

The organizations that thrive will not be the ones with the most advanced models. They will be the ones that learn how to live with an honest mirror without trying to smash it.

Because once the mirror is in the room, pretending it is not there is no longer an option.

Once something in the room cannot look away, neither can the people responsible for what follows.

CHAPTER 9

AI Failure Isn't About AI

THE FAILURE HAPPENS BEFORE THE FIRST LINE OF CODE

Most AI initiatives don't collapse during deployment; they unravel long before reaching that stage. The failure often begins at the spark of enthusiasm, when someone falls in love with an idea, rushes to build a proof of concept, and confuses novelty with readiness. A polished demo gets mistaken for validation rather than an invitation to ask harder questions. Leadership then accelerates the timeline, prioritizing speed and optics over comprehension and behavioral impact. By the time the project is officially launched, its trajectory is already locked in.

This truth is uncomfortable because it challenges a narrative many organizations cling to. That narrative claims AI projects stumble because the technology isn't mature, the models lack reliability, the data is messy, or the tools evolve too quickly. While those factors occasionally play a role, they rarely explain why initiatives collapse.

The deeper reason is far more unsettling: organizations misread themselves. They misjudge how work truly happens under pressure, overlook the inconsistencies in their processes, and underestimate how fragmented their definitions have become. Most critically, they fail to recognize how profoundly human behavior influences every aspect of AI integration.

AI doesn't enter as a neutral instrument; it becomes part of an existing human ecosystem. It absorbs the system's habits, shortcuts, conflicts, incentives, and fears. If that ecosystem is coherent, AI magnifies that coherence. If it's fractured, AI amplifies the cracks. When ambiguity is the glue holding things together, AI exposes that dependency almost immediately.

What organizations often label as "failure" is really exposure, the sudden visibility of weaknesses that were always there. AI doesn't create dysfunction; it reflects and intensifies it. And that reflection is what makes success so elusive for those who misunderstand the system they're trying to transform.

THE PATTERN IS ALWAYS THE SAME

Across industries and organizational levels, the same story unfolds. Someone proposes an idea, often promising, occasionally brilliant. A small team turns that idea into a proof of concept.

It works well enough to impress. Leadership notices, enthusiasm surges, and suddenly the conversation shifts to what AI can accomplish. Momentum builds, and the building begins.

What rarely happens is a pause to confront the uncomfortable questions. Who will actually use this solution? How do those people work today? What habits influence their choices? Which data do they trust, and which do they quietly ignore? Where do definitions clash beneath the surface? What fears will this expose? What long-standing narratives will it disrupt? Which political lines will it cross?

These questions feel inconvenient. They slow progress. They introduce ambiguity. They force leaders to acknowledge blind spots in their own organization. So they are skipped.

Instead, assumptions rush in to fill the gap, assumptions about users, data, processes, adoption, and behavior. The team focuses on delivering outcomes, not on understanding reality.

A product can be built, but that does not guarantee anyone will embrace it. A capability can be delivered, yet fail to change how work gets done. A system can demonstrate value in isolation, only to collapse when it meets the complexity of the organization.

Technically, many AI projects succeed. They generate outputs, answer questions, summarize, classify, predict, and recommend. On paper, the metrics look good.

In practice, adoption splinters. Usage becomes selective. Some teams lean in while others quietly avoid it. Trust erodes. Expectations shrink. What began as a bold initiative becomes a checkbox on a status report.

Pieces of the effort thrive; others falter. Leadership reviews the uneven results and concludes that the technology is not ready. But the truth is more sobering: the organization was never ready.

AI INHERITS THE CHAOS IT IS GIVEN

AI does not introduce chaos; it simply mirrors what already exists. Human systems are inherently tangled. Our language bends under nuance, our decisions are shaped by competing priorities, and meaning shifts depending on context, emotion, and even the moment. Organizations are not precise machines, they are ecosystems built on incentives, survival instincts, and negotiated truths.

Every dataset carries traces of that complexity. Every interaction reinforces it.

When AI enters the picture, it learns from language steeped in ambiguity and bias, from decisions born out of compromise rather than certainty, and from definitions that were never fully reconciled. It consumes documentation that reflects aspirational processes instead of the messy reality of daily work.

None of this stems from malice. Most of it is unconscious. People rarely set out to create flawed data, but good intentions do not erase the patterns AI inherits.

Unlike humans, AI has no memory of consequences, no sense of fear or identity, and no moral compass. It cannot guess why a workaround exists or why a rule was quietly ignored. It sees only the evidence, the patterns embedded in behavior.

This is why the old saying "garbage in, garbage out" misses the point. The issue is not worthless data; it is unexamined behavior. It is behavior in, behavior out.

If those habits are shaped by avoidance, political trade-offs, and inconsistent interpretation, then the outputs will echo those same distortions. AI does not stumble because it is incapable. It stumbles because it reflects the organization as it truly is.

PROCESS INCONSISTENCY IS FATAL

One of the quickest ways to derail an AI initiative is to deploy it in an environment where the same process produces different results depending on who executes it. This is more common than leaders realize. Organizations often have documented workflows, yet the reality on the ground looks very different. Teams interpret steps in their own way, exceptions become routine, and informal knowledge fills the gaps. Work gets done, but not in a uniform manner.

Humans excel at managing this ambiguity. They adjust on the fly, read subtle cues, and compensate for missing clarity. They know which rules bend and which do not, and they understand the unwritten norms that never made it into official documentation. AI, however, lacks that instinct. It cannot intuit context or improvise when the rules are fuzzy. It needs a baseline of consistency to operate effectively. Perfection isn't required, but alignment is.

When processes are fragmented, AI struggles. It cannot guess intent; it can only process contradictions and produce an average of them. Leaders often underestimate how much inconsistency exists because people quietly absorb the friction. The system appears stable only because humans are doing invisible work to keep it functional. Once AI enters the picture, that hidden labor disappears, and the cracks show.

Suddenly, outputs feel erratic. Recommendations clash. Classifications seem off. Summaries miss nuance. The instinct is to blame the algorithm, the data, or the vendor. But the real issue is structural: AI removes the human buffer that was masking dysfunction, and what looked like order reveals itself as chaos.

DEFINITIONS MATTER MORE THAN LEADERS ADMIT

Definitions are more than semantics; they form the backbone of measurement, decision-making, and accountability. When teams interpret the same term in different ways, people can usually navigate the ambiguity. They ask questions, lean on context, and negotiate meaning in real time.

Artificial intelligence cannot do that. It works with definitions exactly as they are encoded and reinforced. When those definitions differ across departments, regions, or roles, the inconsistencies seep into the system. Over time, these contradictions accumulate, making the logic behind classifications, recommendations, and priorities harder to trace. The answers exist, but they are buried beneath layers of conflicting assumptions.

Organizations often respond by imposing uniformity. They publish glossaries, enforce standards, and announce alignment. Yet alignment declared without genuine behavioral agreement is fragile. People may follow the rules publicly while continuing old habits privately. Definitions become symbolic rather than practical. Data appears clean but loses authenticity.

Eventually, what passes for truth becomes a polished version of reality that no longer reflects how things actually work. When AI learns from that distorted truth, its outputs feel disconnected and unreliable. Trust erodes, and the system requires rebuilding.

This cycle persists because the root issue, behavioral misalignment, remains unresolved. Without addressing how people act and interpret meaning, definitions become temporary fixes rather than lasting solutions. The challenge is not simply agreeing on words; it is creating shared practices that make those words real.

THE HUMAN LAYER IS THE REAL DEPENDENCY

AI initiatives often falter because leaders overlook the human dimension. They believe that functional technology guarantees adoption, that resistance signals a need for more training, and that uneven outcomes point to flaws in the model. What these assumptions ignore is that AI does not operate in a vacuum, it intersects with identity, fear, power, and trust.

Employees rarely push back because they lack technical understanding. They hesitate because they understand themselves and the environment they work in. They recognize what vulnerability feels like. They know ambiguity has often served as a shield. They have seen how candor can carry hidden penalties.

Trust in AI reflects the trust that exists among people: conditional, selective, and deeply influenced by psychological safety. When asking questions feels risky, engaging with AI feels risky too. As a result, employees gravitate toward low-stakes uses of AI while avoiding it in critical decisions. They experiment quietly, but hold back when consequences loom large. This is not irrational behavior, it is risk management shaped by organizational norms.

AI adoption struggles not because people are obstinate, but because organizations have yet to earn their confidence. Until trust becomes part of the culture, technology alone cannot close the gap.

ACKNOWLEDGING THE REAL BARRIER

Executives frequently question why their AI initiatives fail to produce meaningful results. CFOs search for the promised value that seems to have vanished. Technology leaders grow weary of what feels like endless "transformation theater," while operations teams wrestle with inefficiencies that never seem to disappear. HR leaders, caught between fear and progress, struggle to explain resistance that decision-makers prefer to ignore.

The root cause is rarely technological. It lies in behavioral readiness. AI mirrors the state of the organization it enters. If the culture is fragmented, AI will magnify that fragmentation. If definitions are inconsistent, AI will embed those inconsistencies into processes. Political friction does not disappear under automation; it becomes more visible. Fear does not originate from AI, it simply uncovers where fear already lived.

In truth, technical breakdowns are uncommon. Human breakdowns are everywhere. Until leadership acknowledges this uncomfortable reality, AI projects will continue to collapse, not because the algorithms failed, but because the organization was unprepared to change.

So the question is not, "What more technology do we need?" The real question is, "Are we ready to behave differently?" Without that readiness, every investment in AI becomes an amplifier of dysfunction rather than a catalyst for progress.

POLITICS, POWER, AND THE ILLUSION OF ALIGNMENT

AI initiatives never start in isolation. By the time an organization decides to adopt artificial intelligence, it already operates within a web of power dynamics, incentive structures, status hierarchies, and long-standing tensions. These forces do not disappear when AI arrives; instead, they are amplified. The technology acts as a catalyst, bringing hidden rules about credit, blame, and authority into sharper focus.

This is why AI projects often become political with remarkable speed. They are highly visible, carry symbolic weight, and represent progress and intelligence in the public imagination. When a tool is linked to efficiency and the future, it inevitably attracts competition, over influence, recognition, and control. AI does not just change workflows; it reshapes the stage where organizational rivalries play out.

EVERYONE WANTS A PIECE OF THE PIE

When artificial intelligence enters the scene, it rarely arrives quietly. Suddenly, every part of the organization feels compelled to stake a claim. Departments seek recognition, executives chase credit, teams lobby for funding, and individuals look for ways to remain relevant. AI quickly becomes more than a technology, it turns into a symbol of influence and status long before it matures into a shared capability.

This isn't pessimism; it's a reflection of how people respond to change. Incentives shape behavior. Metrics define progress. Titles and visibility carry weight. When something powerful and unfamiliar appears, self-preservation and ambition often guide the first moves.

What happens next is rarely a coordinated march forward. Instead, you see a patchwork of initiatives springing up. Multiple proofs of concept tackle similar challenges. Leaders announce competing visions for the future. Teams bypass alignment efforts because they doubt consensus will ever materialize. From the outside, this activity looks like bold innovation. From the inside, it feels more like fragmentation.

Each group crafts its own definition of success, optimizes for its own priorities, and tells a story that fits its perspective. None of these narratives are dishonest, yet none capture the full picture. AI absorbs all these competing agendas, becoming a mirror for organizational complexity.

The outcome? Duplication of effort, inconsistent strategies, and a fog of confusion that masquerades as progress. Momentum is visible, but clarity is not, and that gap can be costly.

OPTICS OVER OUTCOMES

Political behavior flourishes when the stakes feel high, and AI adoption rarely enters under calm skies. It often arrives during periods of urgency, triggered by market turbulence, executive directives, competitive pressure, or boardroom questions that leaders cannot yet answer with confidence.

In that climate, appearances become a form of currency. Organizations rush to showcase demos rather than build resilience. Roadmaps are polished before reality is fully understood. Early wins are amplified to signal momentum, and declarations of readiness surface long before the groundwork is complete.

This creates an illusion of progress. Leadership sees motion, the narrative sounds assured, and the optics suggest transformation. Beneath the surface, however, the fundamentals remain untouched. Behavioral shifts have not taken root. Shared definitions are missing. Processes lack stability. Underlying fears remain unresolved.

AI, in this context, becomes less a capability and more a performance, a carefully staged act designed to reassure. And like any performance, it conceals fragility. The curtain may rise on confidence, but behind it, the foundation is still uncertain.

THE QUIET POLITICS NOBODY WANTS TO NAME

Political dynamics around AI rarely announce themselves loudly; they tend to operate in the shadows. You notice them in passing remarks, in who chooses to join a discussion and who quietly opts out. They surface in decisions about which datasets are shared broadly and which remain guarded, in the subtle divide between those who step forward and those who hold back.

This behavior is rarely about outright opposition. It is a strategy of caution, people preserve flexibility, watch for signals, and wait before committing. Some take matters into their own hands, building tools outside official channels. Others withdraw from the conversation altogether. A few comply on the surface while resisting behind the scenes, while another group charges ahead, betting that speed will outpace unresolved tensions.

Leaders often misread these patterns as resistance to change. In truth, they reflect an instinct to manage risk. The hesitation is not about rejecting AI; it stems from uncertainty, perceived threats to identity, and the fog surrounding future consequences.

FEAR IS THE HIDDEN ACCELERATOR

AI does more than automate tasks; it reshapes the stories people tell about their worth. It uncovers patterns that once stayed hidden and forces uncomfortable questions about judgment, consistency, and performance, questions many organizations have long avoided. Employees sense this shift, even if they struggle to put it into words.

Beneath the surface, there is fear. Fear of being exposed. Fear that data will be misread or weaponized. Fear that transparency will backfire. In many workplaces, honesty carries a quiet cost. Not through formal reprimands, but through signals embedded in culture: promotions that favor certainty over curiosity, evaluations that punish risk-taking, and slogans that encourage questions while rewarding compliance.

In such environments, AI rarely feels like an ally. It feels like a watchtower. Trust becomes conditional. People lean on AI for low-stakes tasks, drafting emails, summarizing reports, brainstorming ideas in private. But when identity, judgment, or career implications enter the picture, they retreat.

From the outside, adoption appears robust. Metrics suggest enthusiasm. Yet beneath those numbers lies a fragile reality: usage is shallow, confined to safe spaces. The promise of AI is vast, but its success depends on more than capability, it hinges on cultures willing to embrace vulnerability without punishment.

WHY ALIGNMENT IS HARDER THAN IT LOOKS

Many leaders assume that alignment happens simply by talking about it. They unveil strategies, circulate guiding principles, and introduce governance frameworks. They set common objectives and expect unity to follow. Yet, when actions fail to match intentions, they are left puzzled.

True alignment is not about agreeing with statements; it is about accepting the consequences tied to them. People commit when incentives are transparent, consistent, and believable. They stay aligned when the cost of ignoring those expectations is tangible and enforced fairly. They trust the system only when vulnerability is not punished.

Absent these conditions, alignment becomes little more than a performance, a show of compliance without substance. And when definitions start to blur, when clarity erodes, the entire structure begins to collapse. That drift is not a minor flaw; it is the point where alignment dies.

WHEN DEFINITIONS BECOME POLITICAL WEAPONS

Definitions are never just technical details; they carry weight. They dictate how success is calculated, what results are prioritized, and who appears competent. When AI projects push for uniform definitions without resolving the deeper disagreements behind them, the tension doesn't vanish, it simply hides.

Teams often adopt the official terminology while clinging to their own interpretations. On paper, metrics seem aligned, yet in practice they drift apart. Data looks tidy, but its meaning begins to dissolve.

AI learns from that fractured reality. Over time, the system becomes opaque, its logic harder to trace. Outputs feel random, decisions seem detached, and leadership starts to question the entire process.

The paradox is striking: the AI fulfilled its instructions perfectly. It absorbed the environment it was given, and in doing so, mirrored its inconsistencies.

MODELS HAVE BACKGROUNDS TOO

One of the least acknowledged realities about AI is that every model carries a history. Its behavior is shaped by the data it consumed or injected, the goals it was built to achieve, and the boundaries set during its design. These elements form a perspective, a lens through which it interprets the world. That perspective often fails to align with the lived experience inside an organization.

When leaders assume AI delivers pure objectivity rather than context-driven insight, friction becomes inevitable. The system seeks patterns that rarely mirror the messy, adaptive ways work actually unfolds. It exposes contradictions people have learned to manage quietly. It revives disputes leaders believed were settled long ago.

Faced with this discomfort, organizations often respond by reshaping the technology instead of themselves. They rewrite prompts rather than rethinking workflows. They layer on controls rather than addressing underlying politics. Each workaround pushes the model further from the truth of daily operations, widening the gap between what is real and what is represented.

THE COST OF PRETENDING POLITICS DON'T EXIST

Ignoring politics does not make them vanish; it allows them to grow unchecked. When leaders frame artificial intelligence as a purely technical challenge, they leave a vacuum where governance should exist. Into that empty space, competing agendas quietly take root. Incentives drift without oversight, and behind closed doors, power struggles intensify.

The result is predictable: resources are consumed, deadlines slip, and teams lose momentum. Fatigue sets in long before progress feels tangible. Eventually, the initiative falters, and leadership labels the effort as premature or incomplete. The cycle resets, waiting for the next trend to arrive.

What changes in the meantime? Very little. Without addressing the political dimension, organizations repeat the same pattern, spending heavily, burning time, and eroding trust, while the underlying issues remain untouched.

WHAT RESPONSIBLE LEADERS DO DIFFERENTLY

Successful AI leadership doesn't erase organizational politics, it works with them. Leaders who thrive in this space make incentives transparent and clarify who owns what. They create environments where disagreements can surface without fear, and they build shared understanding through consistent actions rather than rigid declarations. Restraint and accountability become their tools for reducing anxiety, while trust is treated as something earned over time, never assumed. They accept that control is always incomplete and that clarity can vanish quickly if neglected. Above all, they grasp a critical truth: winning with AI is not a test of raw intelligence, but a measure of organizational maturity.

THE TURNING POINT MOST ORGANIZATIONS MISS

Every AI initiative eventually reaches a crossroads: should the organization prioritize speed or honesty? Chasing performance often feels safer. It delivers quick wins, calms anxious stakeholders, and keeps existing power structures intact. Truth, on the other hand, rarely moves fast. It uncovers gaps, sparks uncomfortable dialogue, and challenges the stories people rely on. Faced with that tension, most organizations lean toward performance, believing it will protect them. Ironically, that choice sets the stage for failure, because ignoring reality always catches up.

BEHAVIORAL READINESS IS THE REAL ARCHITECTURE

By the time an organization officially labels an AI initiative as a failure, the collapse has already been unfolding in silence. It began when excitement was mistaken for comprehension, when rigid definitions replaced shared understanding, and when internal politics were treated as an afterthought rather than a design constraint. It deepened when trust was assumed instead of deliberately cultivated. The truth is, the algorithm didn't malfunction, the surrounding system did. AI didn't create the cracks; it simply illuminated the fractures that were always there.

BEHAVIOR IN, BEHAVIOR OUT

If there is one principle that explains why so many AI projects fail, it is this: the system reflects the behavior it consumes. What an AI produces is inseparable from what it learns, not only from raw data, but from every signal embedded in the environment. Language choices, decision-making habits, feedback loops, incentives, cultural norms, patterns of interaction, even silence and avoidance, all of these shape the model.

Yet organizations often fixate on the visible end of the pipeline: outputs. Are the answers correct? Are the summaries helpful? Are the predictions accurate? When something looks off, the instinct is to tweak the algorithm, retrain the model, or swap it out entirely. But those outputs are only symptoms. They sit downstream from the inputs.

If the behaviors feeding the system are inconsistent, politically charged, fear-driven, or ambiguous, the results will mirror that. Not because the technology is broken, but because it is loyal to its training. AI does not invent coherence; it reproduces what it receives.

This is why AI often feels erratic in certain environments. The issue is rarely technical reliability, it is organizational clarity. Humans instinctively patch over gaps. They interpret nuance, soften conflicts, and apply judgment when rules collide. Machines cannot do this. They do not know which contradictions are trivial and which are catastrophic. They treat every inconsistency as a pattern worth learning.

In short, AI is not unpredictable because it lacks intelligence. It is predictable in the most literal sense: it predicts based on what it has been shown. When the inputs are fractured, the outputs will fracture too. The question is not whether the model works, but whether the organization does.

WHY TRUST DETERMINES EVERYTHING

Trust is not something you install like a feature; it is the environment people operate in. Employees rarely base their confidence in AI on technical specifications alone. Their judgment reflects what the organization has taught them about safety and accountability.

Consider the signals they receive every day: Are questions welcomed or quietly penalized? Does honesty open doors for growth, or does it expose vulnerability? When mistakes happen, are they treated as opportunities to learn or as liabilities to manage? If ambiguity is left to fester, or worse, exploited, then uncertainty becomes the norm.

When asking for help feels risky, engaging with AI feels risky too. If employees suspect that outputs will be used to evaluate rather than assist, they will hold back. If they perceive AI as a surveillance tool instead of a partner, adoption will shrink. This is why trust in AI is never universal; it is situational. People lean on it when the stakes are low, and they avoid it when identity, credibility, or job security are on the line. From a dashboard, usage metrics may look strong. From the ground, the reality is far more cautious.

Organizations often misinterpret this hesitation as a lack of training. In truth, the barrier is cultural. Without trust, no amount of instruction will change behavior. The question is not how well employees understand AI, it is how safe they feel using it.

PSYCHOLOGICAL SAFETY IS NOT OPTIONAL

Psychological safety is often dismissed as an HR talking point, something peripheral to the "real" work of technology and transformation. Yet AI makes it clear that this divide is an illusion. When safety is absent, the promise of AI stalls, not because employees lack capability, but because they lack confidence that their curiosity won't be turned against them.

Adoption falters when people fear that exploring new tools could be misinterpreted, that admitting uncertainty might become a permanent mark, or that asking questions could be seen as incompetence. AI moves faster than most organizational cultures can adapt. It uncovers patterns before leaders have built the guardrails to respond responsibly. In that environment, speed feels less like progress and more like exposure.

But when psychological safety is present, the dynamic shifts dramatically. People lean in. They frame sharper questions, share richer context, and engage with outputs critically rather than passively. They correct errors instead of avoiding the system altogether. Trust doesn't mean blind acceptance; it means confidence to challenge and refine.

That balance, where judgment and trust coexist, is the point at which AI becomes transformative. Without it, acceleration breeds fear. With it, acceleration becomes learning. The question isn't whether safety matters; it's whether organizations can create it fast enough to keep pace with the technology they're deploying.

WHY AI CANNOT FIX DYSFUNCTION

Many people assume that artificial intelligence can tidy up chaotic organizations, bringing order, enforcing uniformity, and erasing inconsistency. The reality is far less convenient.

AI cannot reconcile definitions when people refuse to agree on what those definitions mean. It cannot stabilize workflows that depend on quiet exceptions to keep moving. It cannot override political structures that thrive on fragmentation, nor can it substitute for human judgment in cultures where honesty is penalized.

What AI does accomplish is something more unsettling: it makes dysfunction visible. It strips away the informal fixes and silent compensations that allowed broken systems to limp along. Suddenly, the cracks are no longer hidden, and the work that seemed functional is revealed as fragile.

When leaders encounter this exposure, they often misinterpret it as disruption caused by the technology. But the disruption was always there, AI simply removes the camouflage. It does not create chaos; it illuminates it.

In that sense, AI is not a force of destruction but a mirror. It reflects the truth of how organizations operate, and that reflection can feel uncomfortable because it demands accountability where ambiguity once offered cover.

THE RARE CASE OF TECHNICAL FAILURE

Technical breakdowns are real: systems misfire, configurations go wrong, pipelines collapse, and security gaps appear. Performance can slip, and these issues demand serious technical discipline to fix. Yet, behind every malfunction lies a chain of human choices, compressed schedules, vague accountability, neglected foundations, and incentives that prize speed over resilience. What looks like a technical flaw is often the final symptom of deeper organizational missteps. The visible failure is rarely the origin; it is the echo of decisions made long before the system faltered. If we ignore those roots, we will keep treating symptoms instead of curing causes.

WHAT SUCCESSFUL ORGANIZATIONS DO INSTEAD

Organizations that thrive with AI rarely see it as a temporary project; they approach it as a shift in human behavior. Success begins by observing how work truly unfolds, rather than relying on idealized workflows. They take an honest look at incentives, bring disagreements into the open early, and allow shared definitions to emerge through practice instead of imposing them by decree.

Before scaling technology, they prepare people. They draw clear lines around what AI will and will not influence, clarify who holds control, and show restraint in its application. Accountability is not a slogan but a modeled behavior.

Fear is acknowledged, not brushed aside. These organizations work to minimize risk for employees as much as for systems, making trust an intentional design principle rather than a last-minute communication strategy.

They recognize that AI carries its own history, shaped by training data that may not mirror lived processes. When those differences appear, they treat them as signals, not defects. And instead of forcing the model to conform, they adapt themselves, because alignment is a two-way street.

THE LEADERSHIP SHIFT AI DEMANDS

AI does not call for leaders to be more intelligent; it calls for them to be more transparent. Leadership today cannot rest on the assumption that authority equals understanding. Much of what drives progress inside an organization is hidden, shaped by informal networks, adaptive behaviors, and emotional undercurrents that rarely appear on a dashboard.

True leadership in an AI-driven world means resisting the urge to accelerate simply because speed seems rewarded. It means creating space for listening when everyone expects certainty, and addressing misalignment rather than glossing over it for the sake of harmony.

AI strips away the illusion of ignorance. It exposes contradictions at scale, leaving leaders with a stark decision: maintain the façade of performance or reimagine the system beneath it. That decision will determine whether AI becomes a strategic advantage or a costly vulnerability.

THE REAL REASON AI PROJECTS FAIL

AI initiatives often stumble not because the technology is flawed, but because organizations overestimate their own readiness and alignment. The real obstacles are rarely technical, they emerge from unspoken behaviors, undefined terms, ignored power dynamics, and a lack of trust. When these human factors remain unresolved, even the most advanced systems cannot deliver meaningful change.

This is not a verdict of failure; it is an invitation. Artificial intelligence provides something few tools ever have: a mirror.

It reflects the truth of how work actually happens, how incentives quietly shape decisions, and how culture leaves its imprint on data. It shows what organizations value, and what they avoid.

Those willing to confront that reflection can transform. They learn, adapt, and grow stronger. Those who turn away, however, repeat the same mistakes, only with more sophisticated tools. The question is not whether AI works. It does. The question is whether the organization is ready to see itself clearly and act on what it finds.

WHAT COMES NEXT

If there is one lesson to carry forward from this chapter, it is this: success with AI is not defined by technology alone, but by human behavior. The organizations that will thrive are not those with the most sophisticated algorithms, but those mature enough to apply them with care and responsibility.

Before any system processes data, people create it. Before logic shapes workflows, emotions influence decisions. Consistency cannot simply be enforced; it must be cultivated. Trust, once broken, is difficult to restore, yet it forms the bedrock of every successful initiative.

AI does not eliminate the need for human judgment, it raises the standard for it. And that is why so many AI projects stumble. The failure rarely stems from inadequate technology; it happens because the organization itself was unprepared to change.

AI's Impact on the Unwritten Contract

THE CONTRACT THAT WAS NEVER WRITTEN

Every workplace operates under a silent agreement that no one signs and few ever name. It is not the employment contract, nor the code of conduct, nor the performance review template. Those documents are artifacts, symbols of what leaders hope will be true. They rarely capture the reality of how work unfolds day to day.

The real agreement exists elsewhere. It hides in the spaces between conversations, in the tone of an email, in the questions people stop asking because they've learned the cost of asking them. It shows up in the favors that earn goodwill and the risks that quietly backfire. It is embedded in the shortcuts that become routine and the expectations that hover unspoken.

This is the unwritten contract of work: a web of informal understandings about effort, loyalty, credibility, fairness, and survival. It shapes behavior far more than any official policy. People sense its presence even if they cannot describe it. New hires discover it quickly, not through onboarding slides, but by watching what happens when deadlines slip, when someone works late, when someone doesn't, when a colleague pushes too hard with questions. They learn who gets shielded and who gets singled out.

Every organization has such a contract. Size doesn't matter. Industry doesn't matter. Whether the mission is noble or purely commercial, the pattern persists. The words may change, but the structure remains.

There is what is documented, and there is what is lived. Beneath the surface of formal processes lies a dense layer of unspoken norms: undocumented tasks, private conversations, emotional labor, constant interpretation of signals. Employees often believe they owe more than their job description suggests, flexibility, availability, discretion, silence, extra effort when resources run thin, and a willingness to navigate ambiguity. The phrase "other duties as assigned" stretches far beyond its literal meaning.

In exchange, employees expect something too: fairness, stability, respect, psychological safety, and a reasonable measure of recognition. They hope loyalty is mutual, not one-sided. Yet this balance is fragile, shifting with circumstances, leadership changes, and market pressures. It is never fixed.

The unwritten contract matters because it shapes real behavior, not the slogans printed on posters or the polished statements in leadership decks. It is the hidden framework of organizational life, and anyone who hopes to lead, adapt, or even endure must learn to read it.

Sometimes this contract feels steady. Expectations are clear enough, and the gap between what leaders promise and what employees experience is narrow. People know the rules, even if they are not written down. At other times, the ground shifts violently. Budgets shrink while leaders announce ambitious growth targets. Cultural values are celebrated in speeches, yet rewards flow toward entirely different behaviors. People say one thing and act another. The contract stretches, snaps, and stretches again.

This instability is rarely driven by malice. It is a human response to pressure. Organizations are collections of people navigating uncertainty, and stress bends behavior in unpredictable ways.

What matters most is that the contract never disappears. It governs far more than any documented workflow or system. Leaders often assume that processes define work, but the truth is reversed: behavior defines processes. Before a tool executes a task, emotions, trust, fear, and experience have already shaped how that task will unfold.

That is why the inbox matters, not the software itself, but the exchanges between people. Emails, chats, meeting notes, side conversations, and follow-ups carry the fingerprints of this invisible agreement. You can see it in what gets escalated and what quietly fades away, in the speed of responses to certain names, in who feels safe asking clarifying questions and who does not, and in how decisions are reframed after the fact.

This contract has always been messy. Definitions blur. Processes are improvised. Relationships complicate everything. Emotions seep into decisions whether acknowledged or ignored. For decades, organizations could function this way because fragmentation offered cover. Information was scattered. Visibility was limited. Leaders controlled what was seen, what was measured, and which stories were told about success and failure.

Those gaps created buffers. Contradictions could exist without confrontation. Performance theater thrived. Plausible deniability was baked into the structure. Fragmentation protected authority.

That era is ending.

Artificial intelligence does not invent a new contract. It reveals the one that already exists. By stitching together fragmented data, AI makes the hidden visible, the assumptions, the inconsistencies, the gap between stated values and lived behavior, the difference between how work is described and how it actually happens.

This visibility is not theoretical. It is practical. The context buried in emails, chats, documents, meeting transcripts, and digital traces becomes searchable, comparable, and analyzable. Patterns emerge. Coherence, or the lack of it, becomes obvious. What once required years of tenure to sense can now surface in minutes. Not perfectly, not with full nuance, but enough to spark better questions.

And that shift catches most organizations off guard.

The unwritten contract was never built for scrutiny. It thrived on ambiguity, interpretation, and silence. It relied on the fact that no single person could see the whole picture. AI changes that condition. Suddenly, narrative and information are no longer controlled exclusively from the top. Knowledge moves sideways. Sometimes even upward. Individual contributors gain the ability to interrogate stories instead of merely absorbing them.

This does not grant perfect insight to everyone. But it makes assumptions cheap to test. It makes contradictions harder to hide. Inference becomes easier. And when that happens, power begins to move, not in dramatic explosions, but in subtle, steady shifts.

The unwritten contract starts to strain because the rules it depended on no longer hold. Employees reconsider what they owe the company. They rethink what the company owes them. Leaders feel the tension before they can name it.

Because once the contract becomes visible, it cannot remain unquestioned.

WHEN SPEED BECOMES THE BASELINE

The first disruption AI brings isn't about jobs, it's about expectations. More precisely, it rewrites our old definition of effort.

Before AI became part of daily work, speed carried weight. Delivering quickly signaled competence. Rapid responses suggested dedication. Finishing ahead of schedule was considered exceptional. That entire logic begins to crumble the moment AI enters the picture.

With AI in play, speed stops being impressive; it becomes the baseline. If tasks that once required days now take minutes, the cultural assumption shifts: everything should move faster. Not necessarily better, just faster. And that quiet shift distorts the unwritten contract between employees and organizations.

Workers feel the tension almost immediately. Effort that once earned recognition now feels ordinary. Leaders rarely say this outright, but the expectation leaks through tone, follow-ups, and impatience: We gave you AI, why isn't this done yet?

What gets overlooked in that question is the reality of how AI actually works. Anyone who has used it seriously knows the truth: meaningful results rarely come from a single prompt. They demand iteration, reframing, validation, judgment, and context. AI speeds up certain steps, but it magnifies the thinking work. It doesn't erase it.

Yet from the outside, perception tells a different story. If AI was involved, people assume the human barely worked. The tool gets the credit. The effort disappears. That misconception spreads quickly, and with it, the value of effort erodes. Suddenly, time spent feels suspect. People wonder why something took hours at all. They imagine the human simply accepted whatever the AI produced, no struggle, no discernment, no critical thought.

This assumption is wrong, but it becomes pervasive. And from it emerges a false baseline: a productivity standard that looks achievable on paper but collapses in practice.

Organizations already struggling feel the impact first. AI doesn't repair broken systems; it accelerates them. It generates more output, but not necessarily better outcomes. Requests multiply. Information floods in. Context evaporates.

Those creating content burn out. Those consuming it drown in excess.

The illusion of progress is seductive. At first glance, AI seems to create a workplace humming with productivity, polished reports, rapid responses, endless streams of content. But beneath that surface, something essential begins to erode. The output looks impressive, yet the substance feels thin. Language becomes sleek but hollow. Summaries sound authoritative but lack depth. Stories are shaped to satisfy demand rather than reveal truth.

Over time, this shift hollows out roles. People stop being valued for insight or judgment. Instead, they become checkpoints in a conveyor system: reviewing AI drafts, approving them, passing them along. Next. Next. Next. This is not why organizations hire humans, nor is it what humans excel at. And it certainly isn't what AI was meant to enable. Yet this drift happens when companies confuse throughput with value.

The real problem isn't speed, it's misattribution. AI changes how effort is perceived because it hides the work that matters most: framing, sense-making, deciding what not to trust, knowing when to escalate, understanding consequences. These tasks leave no visible artifacts. They don't show up neatly in dashboards. They live inside judgment. When leaders focus only on the visible output, they stop seeing the invisible contribution. And when employees feel their effort is unseen, their behavior shifts. They stop experimenting. They stop pushing for quality. They avoid intellectual risk. Instead, they retreat into safe patterns, minimal compliance, defensive execution, just enough to avoid scrutiny.

This is how productivity pressure quietly undermines adoption.

At the same time, expectations around availability begin to warp. If AI can run nonstop, the implicit question emerges: why can't people? It's rarely spoken aloud, but the pressure is ambient, shorter timelines, faster responses, more requests, fewer allowances for thinking. The unwritten contract absorbs the message even when leadership never articulates it. You sense it when meetings compress, when follow-ups pile up, when urgency becomes permanent. Eventually, employees internalize the idea that their role is to keep pace with the machine rather than guide it.

That's where trust begins to fracture. Because employees know something leaders often overlook: acceleration without alignment creates risk. Faster dysfunction is still dysfunction. AI doesn't erase accountability. Someone still owns decisions. Someone still absorbs consequences. But when judgment is invisible and effort is devalued, accountability becomes murky. And then a dangerous phrase starts creeping into conversations: "AI said so." That isn't an answer, it's an abdication.

Expertise begins to shift at this point, and not always in healthy ways. Information becomes cheap. Anyone can sound informed. Confidence rises faster than competence. True expertise moves up the stack. It becomes less about producing answers and more about orchestrating systems. The expert is no longer the person playing the instrument; they are the conductor. They interpret upstream signals, anticipate downstream consequences, and understand the context shaping decisions. They know when "good enough" is acceptable and when it is not. AI cannot make that judgment. It can mimic patterns, summarize, and evaluate syntax, but it cannot grasp what is at stake. Someone still has to make that call.

When organizations fail to recognize this shift, they create credibility confusion. People who churn out convincing AI-assisted output gain influence. Those who exercise restraint and judgment appear slow. This inverts the value system. And once that inversion takes hold, fairness comes into question. Why is speed rewarded while care is penalized? Why does volume matter more than consequence? Why is effort assumed to be low when risk is high? These questions rarely surface in meetings. They live in the unwritten contract. They shape trust. They shape retention. They determine whether AI becomes a strategic capability or a wedge that fractures culture.

By the time leaders notice the symptoms, morale has already shifted. The contract no longer matches reality. And AI hasn't created the mismatch, it has simply made it impossible to ignore.

WHEN POWER BECOMES INTERROGABLE

For much of modern organizational history, authority thrived on separation. Leaders operated at a distance, between decision and execution, between raw data and its interpretation, between the official story and the evidence behind it. That gap created space for control. Visibility was curated. Metrics were chosen. Narratives were shaped to define success and failure.

This wasn't always a deliberate strategy; it was a structural reality. Information lived in silos. Systems rarely spoke to one another. Meetings dissolved into memory as soon as they ended, leaving context scattered and incomplete. The entire framework of trust rested on that fragmentation.

Artificial intelligence changes this dynamic. It doesn't deliver perfect transparency, but it stitches together enough fragments to reveal patterns, sometimes coherent, sometimes contradictory. Email threads, chat logs, shared documents, public sources, meeting notes, and the digital residue of daily work begin to align. From these connections, signals emerge.

Leaders can no longer depend on isolation to shape perception. People don't need full access to see the trajectory; they only need enough clues to ask sharper questions. And that subtle shift begins to redistribute power.

It doesn't happen with fanfare. It happens quietly. Individual contributors gain something unprecedented at scale: the ability to verify claims, to check for consistency, to compare what is said in one setting with what appears elsewhere, and to infer patterns of behavior over time.

In this new environment, a different form of capital rises to prominence, credibility. It becomes the currency that matters most, because when information flows more freely, authority is no longer about controlling the story. It is about earning trust through alignment between words and actions.

It is becoming increasingly difficult to hide behind the illusion of performance. Framing reality selectively no longer works as easily. Authority without coherence feels fragile because the structures that once protected it are dissolving.

Artificial intelligence accelerates this shift. It does not recognize hierarchy or titles. It does not distinguish between executives, managers, HR professionals, or frontline employees. It simply amplifies what already exists. That amplification unsettles identity. Leaders sense it first, often without realizing why. There is a quiet disruption when authority becomes something that can be questioned. Imagine someone saying, "AI surfaced this pattern. Can you explain how that aligns with what you just said?" That moment is not about algorithms or dashboards. It is about legitimacy.

And the ripple effect moves outward. It touches peers, middle managers, informal influencers, and long-tenured specialists, anyone whose influence depended on selective visibility. When AI reduces the cost of comparison, authority feels exposed. This is why even modest AI capabilities provoke strong emotional reactions. They reveal inconsistencies. They invite scrutiny. They make questioning easier.

But with this new capability comes risk. In organizations where psychological safety is weak, employees hesitate to challenge authority directly. Instead, they turn to AI as a proxy. They treat it as a neutral voice: "This is what AI shows. What do you say?" When that happens, trust begins to migrate away from human relationships toward machine outputs. And that is dangerous.

AI can detect patterns, but it cannot judge truth. It does not grasp intent, consequence, or harm. It makes assumptions quickly and cheaply. In dysfunctional environments, those assumptions become weapons. People use AI-generated insights to validate grievances. Leaders respond with defensiveness or surveillance. Monitoring expands. Creativity contracts. Trust erodes. This is the fork in the road.

Organizations now face a choice: tighten control or renegotiate the contract. Control feels safe because it is familiar. But it fails. Surveillance destroys trust faster than ambiguity ever did. People stop sharing ideas. They stop experimenting. They stop thinking out loud. Fear replaces collaboration, and the unwritten contract collapses.

Renegotiation is harder. It demands that leaders admit the old rules no longer apply. The previous contract assumed stability, predictable roles, static job descriptions, clear boundaries between decision-makers and executors. AI makes that model obsolete. Jobs are not vanishing wholesale, but they are reshaping continuously. Responsibilities shift. Decision-making blurs. What someone "does here" changes over time.

That reality forces uncomfortable questions:

What does accountability mean when AI participates in every workflow?

What does expertise look like when information is universally accessible?

What does fairness mean when effort is invisible and output accelerates?

What does authority mean when anyone can interrogate the story?

Policies alone cannot answer these questions. They require a new contract, one that explicitly acknowledges AI as part of the system, not just a tool. A contract that redefines value around judgment, context, and consequence rather than speed alone. One that recognizes knowledge as power but treats interpretation as responsibility.

In this new agreement, leaders do not hoard clarity; they create it. They do not rely on ambiguity to maintain control; they build trust networks resilient enough to withstand transparency. They abandon performance theater because coherence matters more than optics. They design incentives that reward judgment, not just throughput. They treat psychological safety not as a soft value but as a structural necessity. They communicate openly about how roles will evolve and why continuous learning is no longer optional. And they involve employees in shaping how AI is used, rather than imposing compliance from above.

Because workers will not accept a contract that extracts value without acknowledging contribution. They will not tolerate surveillance in place of trust. They will not remain in systems that treat them as interchangeable validators of machine output. They will adapt, or they will leave.

The unwritten contract has always existed. AI did not create it. AI exposed it. The organizations that thrive will be those that recognize this moment for what it truly is: not a technology transition, but a renegotiation of how work, power, and trust function. Everyone has a role in that negotiation. And the terms are changing whether leaders participate or not.

That is the reality of the new workplace contract.

CHAPTER 11

AI As a Mirror

THE MIRROR NO ONE ASKED FOR

Most executives assume AI will enter their organization like any other technology: install it, configure it, connect it to data, and wait for answers. That assumption is misleading. AI does not simply integrate into a technical framework; it steps into a human ecosystem. And that difference determines whether everything that follows succeeds or collapses.

AI does not first appear in architecture diagrams or system dashboards. It shows up in the places where work actually lives, your inbox, your shared documents, your meeting notes. It surfaces in late-night emails drafted under pressure, in files edited repeatedly until someone feels safe enough to share, in transcripts where decisions are implied rather than declared, and in messages filled with hesitation, escalation, or quiet withdrawal.

Those spaces are far from neutral. They carry emotion, politics, fear, incentives, and the weight of history. AI does not create these dynamics; it begins to observe them. That is why the metaphor of a mirror matters. When AI reflects, it does not invent new truths. It exposes what already exists, the patterns of perception, self-protection, decision-making, and power navigation that shape human behavior.

Unlike people, AI has no self interest to defend. It does not argue, seek validation, or protect its reputation. It simply reveals what is present. What happens after that reflection is entirely in human hands. And that is where discomfort begins. Leaders often respond as if AI is passing judgment, but it isn't. It does not accuse; it correlates. It aggregates signals and uncovers patterns across volumes of material that no individual could synthesize with the same neutrality or endurance.

The value of this mirror lies not in perfection but in its absence of pride or bias. That very quality, its ability to reflect without self-interest, makes it unsettling. When AI holds up a mirror, it does not change the truth; it changes our ability to ignore it.

WHAT THE MIRROR IS ACTUALLY REFLECTING

To understand why artificial intelligence often feels unsettling, you first need to grasp what it truly reflects. AI is not simply processing raw data; it is echoing patterns of human behavior encoded as information, our word choices, the way we frame issues, the definitions we adopt, and even what we choose to ignore. Every decision to document or dismiss something becomes part of that reflection.

Humans rarely operate with perfect knowledge, and that is not a defect but a fundamental reality. We infer, we speculate, we fill in blanks, and we act on fragments of information long before reason fully engages. AI mirrors this same process. When a prompt assumes a cause, the system accepts that premise. When a report frames a challenge as a timing issue rather than a policy issue, the logic shifts accordingly. Ambiguous language produces ambiguous results, while disciplined framing sharpens the output.

This is why many people misinterpret what they see. They assume AI introduces bias, when in truth it reveals the bias already embedded in the source material. The shock comes from encountering their own assumptions rendered with clarity. Unlike human conversation, AI does not soften or cushion those assumptions; it reflects them back in polished, fluent language.

That fluency is where the real risk lies. When something sounds authoritative, it is easy to mistake reflection for judgment or truth. AI does not add distortion, it amplifies what was implicit all along. The mirror is not emotional, nor is it forgiving. It simply speaks in a tone that feels definitive, and that can be dangerous if misunderstood.

So the discomfort is not about what AI invents, but about what it exposes. It shows us the structure of our thinking without the usual human filters. The question is not whether AI is biased, but whether we are ready to confront the clarity of our own patterns when they come back to us without disguise.

WHY SEEING YOURSELF IS SO UNCOMFORTABLE

One reason artificial intelligence evokes such intense reactions is that it compresses the gap between how people see themselves and the patterns their actions reveal. For years, individuals have shaped their own narratives, choosing which reports to share, framing presentations carefully, selecting metrics that reinforce credibility. Identity has always been curated through deliberate storytelling.

AI interrupts that process. It reconstructs narratives from the raw material provided and the questions asked, not from what someone hoped would remain hidden or highlighted. With only a few queries, it can uncover links and contradictions that were never intended to coexist in plain view.

That is where the emotional turbulence begins. The first wave is surprise, often genuine shock, when years of emails, documents, and decisions are distilled into a single, coherent storyline. Then comes unease, sometimes anxiety, even a sense of vulnerability, because what emerges is not just a record of performance but a reflection of identity. Every judgment, every risk, every choice becomes part of the picture.

The most frequent response? Defensiveness.

"This is wrong."

"AI doesn't understand."

"That's not the real story."

Accuracy becomes the battleground. Yet the real issue is not whether AI is flawless, it rarely is, but whether its interpretation is completely off the mark. Most of the time, it isn't. If a human investigator reviewed every message, every file, every transcript, would they reach similar conclusions? Often, yes. Pattern recognition is not new; it has been the foundation of investigative work for centuries. AI simply accelerates and democratizes that capability.

And therein lies the discomfort: accessibility. What once required weeks of meticulous review now happens in moments, triggered by a single question. That speed erases the buffer of plausible deniability. Suddenly, the story people thought they controlled is reframed by an impartial system, and that loss of control feels deeply unsettling.

WHY THE MIRROR MATTERS ANYWAY

The mirror was never the issue. It simply reflects what has always been there, the unspoken reality of how work truly operates. For many organizations, this reflection is the first authentic signal they have ever received.

Artificial intelligence does not repair these dynamics; it exposes them. It uncovers what leaders could not see, what they chose not to see, or what no one dared to share. Not because of malice, but because people adapt to survive. They shield themselves, manage uncertainty, and shape stories to fit within flawed systems.

Visibility changes everything. When behavior becomes clear, it becomes something that can be intentionally shaped. But this transformation does not come from rigid mandates or colorful dashboards. It begins with understanding the forces that drive action, fear, incentives, and meaning. That is where interpretation matters most. And in that space, real leadership finally takes root.

THE TWO SYSTEMS EVERY ORGANIZATION PRETENDS ARE ONE

Organizations already know they operate on two systems, even if they rarely hold both in view at the same time. One is the official account, the version that can be documented, measured, and defended. The other is the one that actually moves work forward under pressure. The distinction itself is not the issue. The consequences of ignoring it are.

These systems diverge most clearly in the everyday traces people leave behind. In how requests are phrased when certainty is missing. In how responsibility is hedged when risk feels uneven. In who is included when protection matters more than speed. In what goes unsaid, delayed, or quietly rerouted to keep work moving without attracting attention. None of this contradicts the formal system on paper, but it regularly bypasses it in practice.

As long as this gap remains diffuse, it is easy to live with. Each moment can be explained on its own. Each exception can be justified locally. What changes when AI enters is not behavior itself, but its persistence. Patterns that once dissolved into context begin to hold together. The organization is no longer comparing intention to outcome, but design to reality. Whether that exposure clarifies or destabilizes depends on how willing leaders are to accept which system has truly been in control all along.

WHY AI IS USUALLY POINTED AT THE WRONG REALITY

Most AI projects start with a flawed premise: they assume the official documentation reflects reality. Leaders upload policies and wonder why employees ignore them. They feed workflows into models and ask where the process breaks. They share performance metrics and question why results don't align with intent. Beneath all these questions lies a belief that the documented system is the truth, and human behavior is the exception.

That belief is upside down. What people actually do is the truth. The written system is an aspiration, a sketch of how things should work rather than how they do. When AI is trained or prompted as if that documented layer is complete, it ends up learning an organization that exists only on paper, the org chart version, the policy version, the neat and tidy version that ignores the emotional, political, and environmental forces shaping daily decisions.

This misunderstanding explains why so many AI deployments disappoint. It's not because the models lack intelligence or the technology is immature. The real issue is that AI is aimed at the wrong layer of reality. Once you recognize that, the common complaints suddenly make sense:

"AI doesn't understand our culture."

"Its recommendations would never work here."

"It's technically correct but practically useless."

AI is not failing; it is faithfully optimizing for the organization you claim to have, not the one people actually inhabit. Until we bridge that gap, between the imagined system and the lived experience, AI will keep producing answers that look perfect on paper yet fall apart in practice.

WHERE THE BEHAVIORAL SYSTEM ACTUALLY SHOWS UP

The behavioral operating system isn't theoretical, it's visible if you know where to look. It hides in the rhythm of conversations: the person who answers with two words versus the one who writes a page, the tone that leans toward certainty or hedging, the voices that jump in first and those that wait until the dust settles. Influence shows up in subtle ways: whose statements are accepted without proof and who must attach three documents to be taken seriously.

Power leaves its fingerprints too. Look at who gets added to a thread, who disappears without explanation, and who suddenly enters when risk begins to rise. Silence rarely means absence; more often, it's a deliberate signal.

Time tells its own story. Delayed replies, sudden bursts of urgency, threads that fade without closure, and decisions that stall until they quietly become someone else's burden, all of these are patterns worth noticing.

Emotional labor is another layer. People spend energy smoothing rough edges, reframing bad news, softening language, and managing perception instead of tackling the real problem. None of this complexity fits neatly into a process map.

Yet every trace of it lives in the inbox. AI excels at detecting these patterns, once it has access. The challenge is that most organizations refuse to acknowledge this reality. They dismiss the inbox as clutter rather than a rich source of behavioral data. As a result, AI is asked to interpret human behavior while being denied the very signals that reveal how work truly happens.

WHY DEFINITIONS FRACTURE ACROSS THE TWO SYSTEMS

One of the most striking patterns AI uncovers is how definitions drift over time and across teams. Words that appear simple and universal, terms like "done," "urgent," "approved," or "high priority", rarely carry the same weight in every context. On paper, these labels look standardized. In reality, they are fluid.

Formal systems assume definitions are fixed and stable. Yet in day-to-day operations, meaning is constantly renegotiated, shaped by deadlines, trust, and incentives. AI makes this tension visible because it aggregates language from multiple environments. It detects that "approved" in one workflow signals completion, while in another it merely opens the door to three more steps. It notices that "urgent" can mean "drop everything immediately" in one setting but only "please confirm receipt" in another. Even phrases like "looks good" oscillate between genuine approval and polite disengagement.

Humans manage these inconsistencies instinctively, smoothing over gaps without conscious effort. AI, however, exposes them in stark detail. That revelation often feels uncomfortable because it shows that misalignment isn't rooted in technology, it stems from behavior. Coordination falters not because systems fail, but because shared language fractures under competing pressures. When AI highlights these cracks, it forces organizations to confront the human side of alignment.

WHY LEADERS ARE OFTEN SURPRISED BY WHAT AI REVEALS

Leaders often claim they are caught off guard by what AI reveals. Yet the novelty rarely lies in the behavior itself, it lies in the sudden clarity. For those who truly understand the pulse of their organization, most AI-driven insights should feel familiar. They might stir discomfort or confirm suspicions, but they should not seem foreign.

When surprise occurs, it usually signals a gap. A gap between leadership and the realities faced on the front lines. A gap in understanding how work actually flows through the system. A gap in recognizing the quiet strategies employees use to cope and keep things moving.

AI closes those gaps with remarkable speed. It does not wait for agendas or approvals; it simply mirrors the patterns that exist, whether or not they fit the story leaders prefer to tell.

This is why some leaders describe AI as illuminating, while others see it as unsettling. The difference is not about rank or authority, it is about closeness. Leaders who stay near the lived experience of their teams find AI affirming. Those who operate at a distance often experience it as a challenge to their narrative.

WHAT THE TWO SYSTEMS MEAN FOR AI DESIGN

Designing AI solely around documented processes often produces solutions that appear polished but collapse when applied in real-world conditions. On the other hand, giving

AI unfiltered access to human behavior without interpretation risks turning observation into judgment. Neither extreme succeeds.

AI must engage with reality rather than idealized aspirations, yet its reflections require human framing to make sense. Behavioral systems reveal the reasons behind actions, they clarify, not justify. Ignoring these dynamics does not erase them; it simply ensures flawed conclusions.

AI cannot close the gap between formal rules and lived behavior. What it does is expose that gap. The critical question is how we respond to this visibility: do we use it as an opportunity to learn and adapt, or as a mechanism for control and punishment? That choice determines whether AI becomes a catalyst for growth or an instrument of enforcement.

CONTRADICTIONS, BLIND SPOTS, AND THE MOMENT OF BEING SEEN

One of the most profound shifts AI introduces within an organization isn't simply about making predictions or automating tasks, it's about uncovering connections. AI stitches together fragments of human activity that were never intended to coexist in a single frame. A casual email from last spring, a hurried message sent under stress, a document tailored for a specific audience, even a meeting transcript where tone carried more weight than the actual words, all of these pieces suddenly converge.

People have always been aware these fragments existed, scattered across time and context. What they lacked was the ability to weave them into a coherent picture without shaping the story themselves. AI removes that barrier. It assembles the mosaic without permission, without narrative filters, and in doing so, it changes not just what we know, but how truth inside an organization is constructed.

THE EMOTIONAL REACTION TO BEING SEEN

Emotional reactions tend to unfold in a recognizable order. The first wave is surprise, sometimes bordering on shock, especially when the sheer volume and clarity of the material presented feels overwhelming. What unsettles people initially is not the insight itself, but the precision with which it has been articulated.

That clarity often gives way to unease. A creeping sense of exposure emerges: choices you made, patterns you reinforced, narratives you trusted now appear under a sharper lens. This discomfort frequently evolves into defensiveness, expressed through statements like, "This is wrong," or "AI doesn't understand the full picture," or even, "That's not how it really happened."

These objections are not without merit. Context does matter, and interpretation can shift meaning. Yet the real issue is rarely about perfect accuracy. Instead, the question becomes: is the reflection completely off base? In most cases, the answer is no.

Imagine someone reviewing every email, message, document, and transcript you've ever produced. Would they arrive at similar conclusions? Often, yes. What AI introduces is not a new concept but an acceleration of an old one, pattern recognition has always been part of investigative and forensic work. The difference now is speed, and with speed comes the erosion of plausible deniability.

That erosion matters. Plausible deniability has long served as a quiet stabilizer within organizations, allowing ambiguity to soften accountability. When AI removes that buffer, the dynamics of organizational life shift in ways that feel sudden, even inevitable.

WHY DEFENSIVENESS IS SO COMMON

Defensiveness rarely signals guilt; it usually signals a perceived threat. When artificial intelligence enters the picture, it often challenges identity before it ever touches performance. People instinctively guard the version of themselves they believe to be true. Leaders cling to authority, teams fight to remain relevant, and shared narratives become shields for psychological safety.

When AI mirrors human behavior without softening its tone, the feedback can feel like an accusation, even when no judgment exists. For some, this sparks embarrassment or vulnerability, a quiet recognition that not everything can be denied. For others, it brings validation and relief, as if a long-hidden truth finally has language.

Both responses can coexist. What determines whether this moment becomes a catalyst for growth or a source of harm is what happens next.

ORGANIZATIONAL MATURITY DETERMINES THE OUTCOME

When organizations acknowledge that people make mistakes, blind spots stop being liabilities and start becoming opportunities. Curiosity replaces blame, and the question shifts from "Who caused this?" to "What can we learn?" Reflection becomes a tool for growth rather than a trap for judgment.

In contrast, fear-driven cultures twist the same insight into a weapon. What could have sparked dialogue instead becomes surveillance. Interpretation hardens into verdicts, and technology, especially AI, turns into an extension of authority rather than a partner in progress.

The irony is striking: AI doesn't create dysfunction; it simply illuminates what was already there. Leaders often find themselves unsettled not by new behaviors but by the sudden transparency. What was once whispered in private now appears in plain view, and that visibility shifts power in unexpected ways.

The real disruption isn't the data itself, it's the fact that everyone can see it. And that changes the game entirely.

WHY BLIND SPOTS WERE INVISIBLE UNTIL NOW

Blind spots endure because organizations often prize harmony over accuracy. When a narrative feels socially intact, it tends to persist. Metrics that appear reasonable rarely invite deeper scrutiny. Contradictions remain scattered, unconnected, until someone, or something, threads them together.

AI performs that stitching. It does not pause to ask if you are prepared for the pattern it reveals. The experience of recognition can feel overwhelming, as if time, distance, and control collapse into a single, unflinching image.

The mirror offers no malice, only neutrality. The real question is whether the organization can withstand that clarity without fracturing under its own weight.

WHAT THE MIRROR MISSES, AND WHY OBEDIENCE IS DANGEROUS

For all its precision, AI cannot grasp context in the way humans do, and that gap is permanent. It isn't a flaw waiting to be fixed; it's a boundary that defines what AI is and what it is not.

Unlike people, AI enters the world without history. It carries no scars from past mistakes, no memory of speaking out and paying the price, no experience of weighing honesty against survival. It has never faced the quiet calculation of whether to protect a job, a team, or a reputation. Those lived realities shape nearly every human exchange in the workplace.

Organizational language rarely speaks in absolutes. It bends and adapts under pressure. It signals risk as much as meaning. A phrase like "Quick sanity check" often masks a need for cover. "Looks good" might signal approval, or indifference. "Can you take a look" is less a question than a polite directive. Humans decode these signals because they share the same environment of constraints and consequences. AI, by contrast, sees words, not the weight behind them.

Even when AI attempts to infer intent, that guess should be treated as provisional, not definitive. Context is not embedded in syntax; it lives in shared experience, in norms that evolve inside teams and organizations.

This is where many companies stumble. They assume that language is literal, that meaning can be extracted like data. But meaning is negotiated, shaped by risk and trust. Without acknowledging that, organizations risk building systems that read the words yet miss the story.

THE DIFFERENCE BETWEEN REFLECTION AND AUTHORITY

A mirror reflects what stands before it; it never chooses what to show. When leaders start treating AI outputs as commands rather than signals, they hand over authority to something that cannot be held responsible. That transfer feels like progress, efficient, impartial, even safe, but those impressions are illusions.

Following AI blindly often means following your own assumptions, polished and returned in fluent language. The way you frame a question shapes the answer. The premises you embed dictate the logic that comes back. Vague framing produces vague results. Dysfunctional questions breed dysfunctional solutions. What goes in is what comes out, only louder.

This is how organizations end up scaling their worst habits. Broken incentives harden into systems. Misleading metrics gain a veneer of legitimacy. Cultural avoidance accelerates faster than any formal process ever could.

Obedience does not clarify; it amplifies. And amplification without accountability is dangerous. AI cannot own consequences. Humans can, and must. That difference is not abstract theory; it is the foundation of operational integrity.

WHY AI SO OFTEN GETS BLAMED FOR HUMAN FAILURES

When AI-driven recommendations fall short, leaders often assume the technology itself is flawed or unreliable. In reality, the breakdown usually lies in how its output is interpreted.

Organizations frequently aim AI at documented processes and expect it to explain real-world behavior. They ask it to optimize theoretical models while people are navigating practical constraints. They expect it to read silence without grasping the fear behind it, or to diagnose delays without recognizing the weight of overload and risk avoidance.

AI may label something as a delay, but humans often understand the reasons behind it. When leaders treat AI's conclusions as unquestionable truth, they end up penalizing individuals for adapting to systems that were never designed for reality. However, when those same insights are treated as the beginning of a conversation, they reveal the hidden pressures and limitations shaping human decisions.

The gap isn't about intelligence; it's about stance. Technology offers signals, but meaning emerges only when interpretation invites dialogue.

WHY CONTEXT CANNOT BE OBEYED

Context isn't just a list of rules. It's shaped by people, their relationships, past events, motivations, and the results of their actions. AI can point out clues that help us understand this, but it can't take responsibility for what those clues mean or what should happen next.

Intent makes things even trickier. At work, people rarely say exactly what they mean. A "yes" might be clear, or it might only be hinted at. Someone who seems to agree could actually be checked out. Silence can mean anything, from agreement to fear to exhaustion. AI can spot these patterns, but deciding what to do about them is up to humans.

The real risk isn't that AI makes mistakes. It's that people stop thinking for themselves. When leaders rely on AI outputs instead of their own judgment, they give up responsibility while pretending to be objective. That erodes trust faster than any tech failure. People notice when decisions are passed through a tool to avoid accountability.

THE COST OF TREATING THE MIRROR AS A VERDICT

When organizations treat AI as an unquestionable authority, they transform reflection into a weapon. What should spark curiosity instead becomes a tool for accusation. Patterns are no longer insights; they turn into punishments. Learning shifts from growth to surveillance, and that is the breeding ground for ego-driven conflict.

The irony is that many companies believe this approach signals discipline and data-driven rigor. In reality, it institutionalizes fear. It rewards obedience rather than comprehension and perpetuates the same dysfunction that AI was meant to illuminate.

The damage does not come from the mirror itself, it comes from how its image is interpreted.

AI's greatest value lies in its ability to expose risk without assigning guilt, to highlight contradictions without dictating consequences, and to open doors for inquiry rather than slam them shut. That kind of environment demands leaders who can resist the urge for quick judgment and embrace complexity.

The question is not whether AI can reveal uncomfortable truths, it can. The real challenge is whether leadership has the maturity to turn those truths into dialogue instead of dogma. Without that, technology becomes less a tool for progress and more a mechanism for control.

INTERPRETATION IS LEADERSHIP

A mirror can show you what's there, but it can't fix anything. That's where many leaders get stuck, they think seeing the problem is the same as solving it.

AI is great at spotting patterns, risks, and inconsistencies faster than any team could. It can pull together years of behavior into a clear picture. It can highlight where stories don't match facts, where incentives push people in the wrong direction, and where fear quietly influences decisions.

But AI can't tell you what those things mean. That's not its job. That's yours.

Making sense of what you see isn't a technical task. It's a human one. It takes judgment, context, ethics, and an understanding of consequences, things AI will never have.

This is the point where organizations either grow stronger or start to break apart.

WHY INTERPRETATION IS NOT OPTIONAL

When leaders treat AI results as final answers, judgment gives way to blind compliance. It can look efficient, even safe, like progress on paper. In reality, it's surrender.

Handing authority to a system without taking responsibility for its consequences doesn't just weaken leadership; it destroys trust faster than uncertainty ever could. People notice when decisions are pushed through technology to dodge accountability. They sense it immediately. And once that trust is gone, accuracy alone cannot restore it.

AI can reveal patterns, but it cannot decide what those patterns mean or how to act on them responsibly. That gap, the space between information and interpretation, is where leadership either prevents harm or creates it.

WHAT RESPONSIBLE INTERPRETATION LOOKS LIKE

Responsible interpretation begins with how we position ourselves. Leaders don't rush to ask, "Is this correct?" but instead wonder, "What story might this data be telling?" Certainty is rarely the goal; understanding the surrounding context matters far more. Outputs should not be treated as final verdicts but as working hypotheses that invite exploration.

Curious leaders dig deeper: What incentives shaped these actions? What limitations were people navigating? How did the presence, or absence, of psychological safety influence their decisions? Every behavior has roots, and those roots feed the system. When fear, overload, or misalignment drive the inputs, AI will inevitably amplify those same patterns.

Interpretation, then, is not about enforcement; it is about learning. It transforms reflection into insight, helping organizations see beyond surface-level results and uncover the conditions that produced them. In doing so, leaders create space for growth rather than punishment, and for adaptation rather than rigid control.

WHY THIS IS A LEADERSHIP TEST, NOT A TECHNOLOGY TEST

AI does not create cultural maturity; it simply exposes whether it is present. In organizations where emotional intelligence runs deep, artificial intelligence becomes a catalyst for learning and alignment. Leaders treat new visibility as an opportunity to coach, to uncover blind spots without fear, and to address recurring patterns without assigning blame. The goal is to reduce friction, not tighten control.

Contrast that with environments lacking maturity: the same transparency morphs into surveillance, reflection becomes ammunition, and insights fuel ego battles. The technology itself remains neutral, yet its impact shifts dramatically depending on leadership behavior. When accountability feels threatening, AI becomes a weapon. When accountability feels natural, it becomes a liberating force. The real divide is not about technical skill, it is about the willingness to embrace responsibility.

THE SYMBIOTIC LINE THAT CANNOT BE CROSSED

The future of work will not be defined by a battle between humans and AI, but by how well they complement each other. People bring depth, meaning, judgment, and accountability, while AI contributes precision through patterns, clarity, and consistency. When these strengths align, organizations gain insight without sacrificing their human core. When they blur, automation amplifies existing flaws instead of solving them.

AI's role is not to deliver final answers but to spark better questions. It should open dialogue, highlight risks, and illuminate possibilities rather than dictate decisions. Think of it as a mirror: it reflects reality faithfully, yet leaves the interpretation, and the choice of who to become, entirely to us.

SEEING CLEARLY CHANGES EVERYTHING

When behavior becomes visible, it turns into something we can shape. Not by issuing commands or flooding dashboards with metrics, but by creating environments where incentives align, safety is assured, and work carries meaning.

AI offers organizations a rare gift: a clear, unfiltered view of how work truly happens. That clarity is unsettling because it exposes realities we often prefer to ignore. Yet discomfort is the price of progress, and this truth cannot be avoided.

The leaders who thrive in this era will not be those who rush to deploy technology or chase automation for its own sake. Success belongs to those who can face the reflection without denial, interpret it with care, and accept responsibility for what follows.

The mirror is already in place. The real question is not whether you approve of what you see, but whether you have the courage to lead after seeing it.

CHAPTER 12

AI Replaces Behaviors, Not People

THE CATEGORY ERROR THAT KEEPS DERAILING THE CONVERSATION

Conversations about AI and the workplace often begin with a familiar question: Which jobs will disappear? At first glance, it feels like the right starting point, practical, responsible, even strategic. But that question quietly frames the entire discussion in a way that misleads us before we've even begun.

Jobs are not the true measure of change. They never have been. A job is simply a label, a convenient container that helps organizations manage charts, pay scales, and headcount. It is not where the essence of work resides.

Work exists in actions, in behaviors, in the way tasks are carried out. Until leaders recognize this distinction, every conversation about automation will lean toward anxiety rather than understanding. If we keep focusing on job titles instead of the underlying behaviors, we risk planning for the wrong future.

WHY "JOB REPLACEMENT" IS THE WRONG LENS

When most people hear the word "job," they picture something neat and contained, a role with a clear mission, defined duties, and a stable identity. That image feels natural because it mirrors how organizations describe themselves on paper.

Yet, when you observe how work actually happens inside those same organizations, that tidy picture dissolves almost instantly. What emerges instead is a web of small, shifting actions: drafting a message, reviewing a document, hunting for information, summarizing findings, scheduling meetings, translating jargon, clarifying intent, following up, deciding what matters now and what can wait, and plugging gaps no one officially acknowledged.

These actions are fluid. They bend and reshape under pressure. A new executive steps in, and suddenly the same position demands more documentation, more reassurance, and more storytelling. A regulatory change sneaks in, and extra steps appear that never make it into the official workflow. A new system launches, and quietly, people find workarounds to keep momentum alive.

The job title remains unchanged, but the behaviors underneath it keep evolving. That isn't dysfunction, it's resilience. Organizations endure because people adjust long before anyone redraws a process map or updates a role description. The distance between what's written and what's lived isn't a flaw; it's the reality of modern work.

And this shifting space, the gap where adaptation happens, is precisely where AI steps in.

RESHAPING OF JOB DUTIES

A job isn't just one thing you can swap out. It's a mix of tasks and habits built up over time. Some of those tasks are simple and repeat often. Others are messy and unpredictable. Some are low-risk, while others are critical to keeping everything running. Certain tasks exist because the system needs them, and others exist because the system doesn't work perfectly.

That difference matters.

When AI starts writing emails, summarizing meetings, creating status updates, organizing requests, or turning notes into slides, it's not replacing the whole job. It's handling the parts that are easy to repeat and don't carry big risks.

This is why AI feels both helpful and a little unsettling. Helpful, because it takes care of the boring stuff. Unsettling, because something familiar changes. But just because something feels familiar doesn't mean it can't be replaced.

The first tasks AI takes on aren't the ones that define your role. They're the predictable, low-risk jobs that can be automated without changing what the role really means.

That's why the job still exists even when some tasks disappear. And it's why calling this "job loss" gets it wrong. What's really happening is that jobs are being reshaped. The work inside them is shifting, but the role itself remains.

BEHAVIOR VERSUS RESPONSIBILITY

One of the most serious mistakes organizations make is confusing responsibility with behavior. They are related, but they are not interchangeable.

A behavior is an action, something tangible that can be measured and completed. Drafting an email, summarizing a meeting, classifying a request, or scheduling a call are all examples of behaviors. They have clear criteria and an endpoint.

Responsibility, on the other hand, is about owning an outcome. It is not tied to a single task and does not expire when a checklist is complete. Responsibilities endure across projects, systems, and even failures. Someone must ensure leadership stays informed. Someone must safeguard the company against risk. Someone must uphold quality, trust, and continuity.

When things go wrong, a specific behavior may have failed, and a person answers for that failure. But responsibility carries weight beyond tasks, it carries consequence. AI can perform actions, but it cannot assume ownership. It cannot be fired, sued, or blamed. It cannot feel regret. Accountability remains human because consequence remains human.

This is why roles persist even as tasks vanish. The work that survives is not mechanical; it is judgment, escalation, exception handling, and risk management. Roles do not disappear, they concentrate, becoming more critical as automation takes over routine tasks.

WHY AI ENTERS THROUGH ASSISTANCE, NOT AUTHORITY

AI typically enters organizations in the role of an assistant because that feels safe. Assistance is familiar. It offers support without taking control. People ask it to draft, summarize, organize, or highlight, tasks that help humans decide rather than replace their judgment.

This model works because it keeps authority in human hands. If the output misses the mark, someone can fix it. If the tone feels off, it can be adjusted. If something is incomplete, it can be added. Errors are visible and inexpensive to correct, which makes the risk tolerable.

Most organizations stop at this stage, not because technology lacks capability, but because moving beyond assistance means stepping into responsibility. Automation demands precision: clear inputs, predictable outputs, and rules for exceptions. Few roles offer that level of clarity because most work is inherently ambiguous.

Work is shaped by trade-offs, speed against accuracy, cost against quality, policy against reality, short-term risk against long-term risk. These choices are not technical puzzles; they are judgment calls. Humans make them because humans bear the consequences.

THE ILLUSION OF ELIMINATION

This is where the common layoff narrative begins to unravel. When organizations automate a wide range of tasks but keep accountability intact, the job itself doesn't disappear, it becomes heavier. What's left behind is the most demanding work: reviewing instead of creating, making judgments rather than carrying out instructions, explaining decisions instead of simply producing outputs, and catching errors that once were prevented through routine repetition. People shift from being makers to becoming gatekeepers.

The position still exists, and so does the title, but the lived experience of that role changes profoundly. Here's the nuance many leaders overlook: employees were already stretched thin long before AI entered the picture. Backlogs piled up, work spilled beyond formal systems, and invisible labor quietly held everything together. AI didn't invent this reality; it illuminated it.

By stripping away repetitive tasks, automation exposes how much of an organization relied on silent human effort to compensate for structural gaps. That revelation is unsettling, not because it signals mass job loss, but because it challenges deeply held assumptions about how work gets done. The discomfort lies in realizing that efficiency wasn't the norm; fragility was. And now, with AI pulling back the curtain, leaders must confront the truth: the hardest part of the job was never the routine, it was the responsibility.

THE HIDDEN COST OF REMOVING THE TRAINING GROUND

Some consequences take time to surface. Judgment rarely arrives as a finished product; it grows through experience. People develop it by engaging in routine tasks, making minor errors, observing outcomes, and gradually absorbing what "good" looks like in real situations.

When those opportunities vanish without a deliberate redesign of the role, the learning environment disappears too. Many organizations cut junior positions, assuming that greater efficiency has erased the need for them. In reality, what gets eliminated is the foundation for future mastery.

The result is a structure where senior professionals hold concentrated responsibility. Yet when they depart, no one remains who understands how decisions are made under the unique pressures and dynamics of that organization. Even seasoned hires from outside often lack the embedded knowledge, the unwritten rules and contextual judgment, that only come from growing within the system.

This isn't a distant risk; it's a slow-moving one. The absence of developmental roles creates a gap that widens quietly until it becomes critical. By the time the impact is visible, the organization has already lost the continuity that sustains expertise.

WHY FEAR SHOWS UP SO QUICKLY

Fear of AI rarely stems from the idea of losing a job; it often comes from the disruption of habits that once felt secure. People worry about the disappearance of the familiar routes to mastery, the steps that made competence predictable. When those pathways vanish, what remains can feel like pure risk without the safety net of gradual learning. There is also the anxiety of being seen when work that was once invisible becomes measurable and exposed.

Teams often cling to practices they describe as irreplaceable, not because those tasks hold sacred value, but because they carried significance. They were the scaffolding for confidence, the foundation for identity, the proving ground for expertise. Even the smallest routines can matter deeply for these reasons.

AI does not strip away that meaning. Instead, it forces organizations to ask whether roles were ever designed to nurture judgment, growth, and responsibility in the first place.

THE REAL CATEGORY ERROR

AI is not erasing people from the workplace; it is reshaping the predictable patterns within roles that were already in motion. What truly threatens organizations is not the disappearance of jobs but the refusal to evolve. When companies cling to rigid job titles as if they were static containers rather than dynamic sets of behaviors, they misinterpret automation as destruction instead of transformation.

Jobs endure because human work is layered with context, judgment, and physical presence, qualities that resist clean repetition. AI only reaches the tasks that can be standardized and replicated. Once that becomes clear, the debate shifts. It is no longer about whether AI will take jobs away; it is about whether leaders will reimagine work so that when routine behaviors vanish, the essential elements, critical thinking, learning, and accountability, remain intact.

This challenge is not rooted in technology. It is a question of leadership courage and vision. Will organizations redesign roles to amplify what humans do best, or will they allow stagnation to hollow out their workforce? The future of work depends on that choice.

WHAT AI LEARNS WELL, AND WHY THAT IS SO REVEALING

When leaders stop viewing AI as a force that eliminates jobs, a more practical question emerges: What kinds of human actions can AI truly handle well? The reality is far less sensational than headlines imply, yet far more revealing for organizations trying to adapt. AI doesn't replace tasks because they matter less; it replaces them because they follow predictable patterns. That nuance is critical. Predictability, not importance, determines what AI can automate. Understanding this helps explain why AI feels both remarkably capable and surprisingly constrained when applied in real-world business settings.

PREDICTABILITY, NOT INTELLIGENCE, DETERMINES AUTOMABILITY

Many people assume that AI's success signals intelligence. That interpretation makes the technology sound sophisticated and reassures decision-makers that they are embracing something cutting-edge. Yet this view oversimplifies reality.

AI thrives in environments where work is structured and predictable. Tasks that rely on language, follow clear rules, or involve repetitive conversions are ideal. These are areas where "good enough" is a shared understanding, even if never formally documented.

Take email drafting as an example. It's often the first use case because most workplace emails don't demand creativity, they demand sufficiency. A clear format, an appropriate tone, and completeness are what matter. The same principle applies to meeting notes, status reports, and other routine communications. These activities may seem ordinary, but they follow recognizable patterns.

Summarization illustrates this perfectly. Humans learn to summarize early in life: identify the main idea, strip away distractions, and preserve meaning. AI performs well here because the underlying structure is already embedded in human communication.

The same dynamic drives format conversion. Turning notes into slides, transcripts into action items, or code into documentation involves reshaping information without requiring deep judgment. Classification works similarly. Deciding whether something is urgent, assigning it to finance or operations, or determining if escalation is necessary are tasks humans do instinctively, though often inconsistently. AI brings scale and consistency, revealing gaps that people previously absorbed without notice.

This is not a story of machines replacing human insight. It is a meeting point between repetition and pattern recognition. AI succeeds because the rules are already written in the way we work.

WHY THESE BEHAVIORS WERE ALWAYS INVISIBLE

The first tasks AI tends to master are often the ones organizations barely noticed, even though they depended on them every day. These were the quiet connectors, the unseen threads that held everything together. Work that happened in the spaces between official projects: drafting, summarizing, organizing, translating. Essential, yet rarely celebrated or properly resourced.

Over time, these efforts faded into the background. They became assumptions, absorbed into job descriptions without acknowledgment. Instead of recognition, people were rewarded with pressure and fatigue.

AI doesn't invent these tasks; it simply exposes their scale and structure. When automation begins to handle them consistently, leaders are often startled, not because the work is new, but because its weight was never measured honestly. Suddenly, the invisible becomes quantifiable.

This is one of the first unsettling truths automation reveals: the hidden labor that made everything possible was consuming far more time and energy than anyone realized. And now, for the first time, its impact is impossible to ignore.

BEHAVIORAL AUTOMATION AS A MIRROR

As artificial intelligence begins to mirror organizational behavior, it reveals what was once hidden beneath the surface. Processes that were never documented start to appear. Informal fixes and quiet adjustments, long managed by human intuition, emerge as visible patterns.

AI does not judge; it simply reflects what exists. When instructions lack clarity, the results echo that ambiguity. When definitions shift over time, classifications follow suit. And when priorities collide, the system makes those tensions unmistakable.

This is often the point where resistance grows, not because the technology is flawed, but because transparency feels unsettling. For years, people absorbed inconsistencies, smoothing rough edges through emotional effort, mental flexibility, and time. Automation removes that cushion. It operates without empathy or improvisation, adhering strictly to the patterns it detects.

When those patterns reveal dysfunction, the reflection can be uncomfortable. It is like holding up a mirror to a room that has been dimly lit for decades; the details were always there, but now they are impossible to ignore. The challenge is not the algorithm, it is the exposure of truths that were quietly managed by human hands.

WHY AUTOMATION FEELS LIKE JUDGMENT EVEN WHEN IT ISN'T

Many teams respond to AI as though it is grading their performance, but that is not what is happening. AI does not measure quality; it replicates patterns. When its output appears messy or incomplete, the real issue is often that the original inputs were inconsistent all along. People have always compensated for those gaps with interpretation, added context, and extra effort, something AI simply does not do.

This is why introducing AI often sparks resistance. Comments like "This isn't how we really work" or "It doesn't capture our culture" are common. These concerns are valid to a point because context and interpretation do matter. Yet the deeper reality is that AI exposes how much of an organization's success has depended on silent human adjustments.

The reflection feels uncomfortable because it is honest. The technology does not create flaws; it uncovers them. What looks like a failure of AI is often a revelation about the systems we thought were solid.

THE REDISTRIBUTION OF EFFORT

When artificial intelligence takes over routine, predictable tasks, the effort behind them doesn't vanish, it simply shifts. Drafting turns into reviewing, summarizing becomes validating, and organizing evolves into managing exceptions. The nature of work changes from creating output to safeguarding accuracy.

This transition often happens without deliberate planning. Companies celebrate efficiency gains but rarely redesign roles to match the new reality. Expectations linger, and in many cases, they grow: You have more time now, so you can take on more responsibility.

The result is a quiet reversal of priorities. Employees spend less time producing and more time making judgment calls. They build less and evaluate more. For senior leaders, this feels familiar territory. For mid-level and junior staff, however, it can be unsettling.

The tasks that once built confidence and skill disappear, leaving behind decisions with higher stakes and fewer opportunities to learn. Without a training ground, judgment becomes the job, and that can feel like stepping onto a tightrope without a net.

WHY PREDICTABLE BEHAVIORS WERE THE SCAFFOLDING

The routines that AI now automates were never trivial; they were the scaffolding for professional growth. Through drafting and revising, people learned judgment, how tone shaped perception, how unclear phrasing invited risk, and how minor mistakes could snowball into major issues. These experiences built intuition over time.

When those steps vanish overnight, roles evolve faster than the skills that once supported them. New employees are asked to approve outputs they've never created themselves. Junior staff face decisions without the foundation of practice. Senior experts, meanwhile, become chokepoints because they're the only ones trusted to override machine-generated work.

The result is an organization that moves with remarkable speed yet stands on fragile ground. Efficiency rises, but resilience erodes. What happens when the system is tested and the human safety net is too thin to catch the fall?

WHY ORGANIZATIONS MISREAD THIS MOMENT

Early wins with AI often convince leaders that scaling automation will resolve deeper organizational challenges. In reality, those successes reveal something else: predictability was carrying far more weight than anyone noticed. AI thrives in environments where processes are structured and roles are clear, even if that structure is informal. It falters when ambiguity, politics, and shifting accountability dominate the landscape.

When leaders deploy AI into those messy spaces without rethinking how work is organized, frustration is inevitable. People blame the technology. Others blame the workforce. Yet the underlying issue remains untouched. Automation didn't erase the behavioral operating system; it simply illuminated it, like a spotlight on the stage no one wanted to see.

THE REAL SIGNAL IN WHAT AI LEARNS WELL

When AI performs well, it often reveals areas where your organization already operates with consistent habits, even if those habits were never formally documented. Where AI falters, it signals places where human judgment, accountability, and experience still carry the weight. Neither outcome is inherently positive or negative; each simply reflects a different kind of strength.

The real risk comes when we assume these two forces, AI and human expertise, are interchangeable. They are not. AI tends to replicate behaviors rooted in its training data, while people lean on intuition and lived context. When those boundaries are acknowledged, automation becomes a stabilizing tool rather than a disruptive force. Ignore them, and dysfunction grows louder, not quieter.

So the question isn't how much AI can accomplish. It's what kind of organization you truly have, and whether you understand its foundations.

WHAT AI CANNOT REPLACE, AND WHY THAT BOUNDARY EXISTS

Automation has limits that speed, fluency, or polish cannot erase. No matter how seamless the output appears or how persuasive the illusion becomes, something essential remains out of reach. That missing element is not raw intelligence, it is lived experience. Machines operate from data and design; humans carry memories, choices, and a life story. This gap is not a matter of abstract philosophy but a fundamental difference in structure and origin.

TRAINING DATA VERSUS LIVED EXPERIENCE

At first glance, training data and lived experience seem alike. Both involve exposure to events and the formation of patterns. Both leave traces that can be recalled later. Yet beneath that surface similarity, they originate from entirely different sources and are structured in profoundly different ways.

Training data is a record, a snapshot of what occurred. It catalogs language, outcomes, labels, and descriptions. It can indicate whether something succeeded or failed, whether it was urgent or routine, celebrated or criticized. What it cannot convey is the texture of the moment, the sensations, the weight of consequence, the feeling of being there.

Lived experience unfolds in real time, anchored to a person within a specific context. It carries emotion, interpretation, physical strain, and social impact. It changes identity and reshapes judgment. It leaves marks that persist long after the event. When humans encounter reality, they meet resistance:

effort, fatigue, discomfort, and the ripple of social consequence. These forces influence how choices are made in the future.

Training data does not bear that burden. It observes patterns without living through cause and effect. That distinction explains why two individuals can share the same event yet emerge with entirely different lessons. Experience is filtered through values, ambitions, relationships, and history. A model compresses those variations into generalized patterns. That compression is powerful, but it flattens meaning.

And in that flattening, something essential is lost, the depth, the friction, the residue that makes experience transformative.

WHY MEANING CANNOT BE SIMULATED

AI can mimic the way humans speak about meaning. It can craft sentences that sound thoughtful, empathetic, even concerned. But imitation is not comprehension. Meaning is born from commitment, having something to lose, something to protect, something that matters beyond calculation. It grows out of preference and risk, from the weight of consequences that shape future choices.

Humans live with that weight. Loss changes behavior. Failure reshapes how much risk feels acceptable. Responsibility sharpens focus. Emotions like love, trust, and fear bend judgment in ways no algorithm can fully capture. These forces are not patterns; they are lived experiences.

That is why accountability remains a human domain. AI can recommend, predict, and even decide, but it cannot bear the burden of those decisions. It cannot lose reputation or credibility. It cannot be sued or blamed. When outcomes go wrong, the answer is never a machine, it is a person, facing legal, financial, and reputational consequences.

Organizations have always been structured around this truth: systems assist, but humans answer. No matter how advanced technology becomes, the capacity to care, to fear, and to take responsibility is what keeps decision-making human.

EMBODIMENT AS A SOURCE OF JUDGMENT

Judgment is not confined to thought alone; it is deeply rooted in the body. Every moment, humans receive a stream of physical signals, fatigue, hunger, tension, pain, comfort. These sensations are not mere distractions; they are vital data points shaping perception and action.

Such signals alter how risk is evaluated, when decisions are made, and even when something feels wrong before words can explain it. A seasoned officer senses danger before evidence appears. A manager notices a meeting slipping off course before the agenda collapses. A mechanic halts work because a sound feels off. A baker knows the dough is ready by touch alone. These are not random impulses; they are patterns learned through countless experiences and consequences.

Artificial intelligence lacks this dimension. It has no body to sense urgency, no discomfort to trigger caution, no intuitive timing to abandon procedure when reality shifts. This absence explains why rigid protocols often fail in unpredictable environments and why human experts override them, not out of rebellion, but because judgment forged through lived experience demands it.

Emotions, far from being noise, serve as navigational cues. Fear heightens focus. Unease signals caution. Confidence fuels decisive action. These embodied signals steer choices long before conscious reasoning catches up. AI cannot replicate this interplay; it operates without the subtle whispers of sensation that guide human judgment.

WHY ACCOUNTABILITY CANNOT BE AUTOMATED

Responsibility is not a checklist item; it is a bond that connects choices to their aftermath. Every decision casts a shadow, and that shadow is consequence. Authority carries weight because blame follows it. Actions shape reputation, and reputation is what lingers long after the moment has passed.

Artificial intelligence can illuminate possibilities, uncover trends, and offer guidance, but it cannot bear the weight of results. It has no stake, no pride, no memory of failure. That is why the notion of AI as a colleague falters under close examination. A true coworker risks something personal, credibility, trust, even career. A tool does not.

When organizations attempt to grant authority to machine-generated outputs, accountability does not vanish; it simply becomes harder to see. Someone will still answer when things go wrong. And when responsibility is blurred behind algorithms, trust erodes. People recognize when decisions are routed through systems as a shield against ownership, and that recognition breeds doubt rather than confidence.

THE COST OF REMOVING EXPERIENCE FROM THE ROLE

When artificial intelligence takes over the tasks that once defined a role, the role itself doesn't vanish, it transforms. Instead of creating, people find themselves assessing. Instead of building, they spend their time validating, explaining, and defending work produced by systems they didn't control. The craft disappears, and with it, the training ground that once shaped expertise.

Without hands-on practice, judgment becomes fragile. New employees are asked to critique outputs they never learned to produce. Junior staff must make decisions without the foundation of experience. Senior professionals, meanwhile, turn into bottlenecks because they are the only ones trusted to override the machine. What looks like efficiency on the surface hides a structural weakness.

Collaboration erodes as teams shift from co-creation to negotiating trust. Satisfaction declines because the work that remains is the hardest, most stressful part, every day. This isn't a flaw in the technology itself; it's the consequence of failing to redesign the system around it. When roles evolve without rethinking how people grow, organizations trade resilience for fragility.

WHY THIS BOUNDARY MATTERS

AI changes work because behaviors can be mapped and automated. What it cannot replicate are the dimensions of being human, our lived experience, embodied presence, moral judgment, and the sense of meaning that emerges from consequences rather than patterns.

waves of innovation where hesitation proved costly. So when AI enters the narrative, it awakens institutional memory: we cannot afford to miss this one. We cannot be late again. We need evidence of movement.

And evidence becomes the priority. The first signs of AI pressure aren't engineering decisions, they're storytelling decisions. How do we frame this for investors? What internal milestones can we showcase? What signals will convince stakeholders that momentum exists? Visibility becomes the metric long before value does. AI turns into something that must be seen before it is understood, and counted before it truly matters.

WHEN RELEVANCE REPLACES EVIDENCE

Many organizations dive into AI without first defining the real problem they hope to solve. When leaders are asked what issue AI is addressing, the responses often sound lofty but lack precision: modernization, innovation, competitiveness, transformation. These words feel strategic, yet they rarely diagnose anything specific.

Without agreement on what is broken, measuring success becomes guesswork. A pilot might look promising, but no one can pinpoint why. Was it the technology? The quality of data? The oversight from humans? Or did it work simply because a motivated team gave it extra attention? Without clarity, early wins become deceptive. They create confidence without understanding, leaving the organization with validation but no transferable lessons.

This is how the illusion of readiness takes root. Dashboards start appearing. Adoption metrics are tracked and celebrated.

Training completions are highlighted. Tool counts rise. A few workflows get automated. Cost savings are estimated. Sometimes headcount shrinks or vacancies remain unfilled. On paper, progress seems undeniable.

Yet none of these indicators answer the deeper question: Has the way decisions are made truly changed? That question is uncomfortable because it resists neat packaging in a slide deck. It forces reflection on whether AI is shaping judgment or simply decorating processes. Until organizations confront that reality, they risk mistaking activity for transformation.

SCALING THE STORY BEFORE SCALING THE SYSTEM

AI adoption often accelerates not because of its actual capabilities, but because organizations feel compelled to appear active and innovative. The narrative of progress begins to overshadow the reality of impact. Questions like "How many tools have we launched?" or "How many employees have access?" dominate dashboards. Even "How many workflows now claim to be AI-enabled?" becomes a badge of success. These indicators are easy to count, yet they barely scratch the surface. They reveal nothing about the quality of decisions being made, the strain on oversight, or whether people truly know when to question the system's output.

What's missing from these reports is the invisible cost. As AI expands capacity, work tends to cluster around fewer hands. Highly skilled contributors accelerate, while entry-level roles shrink or vanish entirely. Talent pipelines thin, succession planning fades, and institutional knowledge becomes fragile, locked inside a small group operating at AI-augmented speed. Efficiency gains are celebrated loudly, but the erosion of resilience goes unnoticed.

When organizations chase speed and scale without asking what dependencies they are creating, they are not building strength. They are building something brittle. The story of progress may look impressive, but beneath it lies a structure that can crack under pressure. The question worth asking is not "How much have we automated?" but "What happens when the few who hold the knowledge step away?"

THE EARLY SIGNS LEADERS MISS

One of the earliest signs that an organization is unprepared to scale AI rarely comes from technical breakdowns. It emerges from uncertainty in behavior and purpose. When people cannot clearly state what problem AI is meant to solve, the foundation is already shaky. Oversight roles may exist on paper, yet under pressure, no one can describe what "good" performance truly means. The phrase "human-in-the-loop" sounds comforting, but when output grows beyond human capacity, review becomes symbolic. Checks turn into clicks. Throughput replaces judgment.

Defining acceptable failure is another blind spot. For human processes, organizations routinely set error thresholds. AI, however, is often treated as if improvement will happen on its own or that mistakes will announce themselves. At scale, neither assumption holds true. Biases creep in quietly. Faulty logic multiplies. Silent decisions ripple across thousands of customers or employees long before anyone notices. By the time harm surfaces, the system has already reshaped behaviors around its flaws.

This is not negligence. It is the result of incentives pulling in the wrong direction. Speed earns praise. Delivery is visible. Prudence is invisible. When deadlines overshadow outcomes, motion masquerades as progress. The organization accelerates without intention, and once momentum builds, slowing down feels like defeat.

Scaling AI is not just a technical challenge; it is a cultural one. Without clarity, deliberate oversight, and a shared definition of risk, organizations risk building systems that move faster than their ability to steer. The question is not whether AI can work, it is whether the organization can pause long enough to make it work responsibly.

URGENCY IS NOT THE PROBLEM

There is no denying the urgency surrounding AI. To ignore it would be unrealistic. The technology is evolving at a remarkable pace, reshaping capabilities and altering competitive dynamics.

Yet urgency alone does not equal strategy. Acting quickly without discernment is not progress, it is reaction. The real failure isn't speed; it's speed without governance. It's the belief that frameworks, vendors, and tools can somehow offset the absence of clear incentives, defined accountability, and engaged leadership.

AI does not create new risks in isolation. Instead, it magnifies the vulnerabilities organizations already accept, the way decisions are made, responsibility is assigned, and behavior is managed under pressure.

The rush to scale before achieving understanding is not a technological flaw. It is a leadership gap. And that gap becomes visible long before any policy collapses.

So the question is not whether to move fast, but whether to move wisely. Without judgment, urgency becomes a liability rather than an advantage.

THE COMFORT OF PILOTS, TRAINING, AND DASHBOARDS

By the time most organizations begin talking about scaling AI, they usually have a list of reassuring signals. A pilot project showed promise. Employees completed training sessions. Adoption charts look healthy. Executives can confidently say, "We've tested this."

And yet, this is often where progress stalls.

Pilots, training programs, and dashboards all serve a purpose, but they tell a narrow story. They reveal activity, not capability. They show participation, not preparedness. What they fail to capture is judgment, the ability to make sound decisions when AI becomes part of everyday work.

Consider the pilot phase. Success often depends on a controlled environment where motivated teams pay close attention. Exceptions are handled manually. Risks are absorbed quietly. Oversight is generous because the volume is low. These conditions create a bubble of success that rarely survives real-world pressure.

When the same system moves into production, the context changes dramatically. Workflows accelerate. Metrics matter. Oversight thins out. People lean on AI outputs more than they intended, and inconvenient edge cases are ignored. The technology hasn't changed, but human behavior has.

Training faces a similar blind spot. Most programs teach what the tool can do, not how to think critically about its use. Completion rates are tracked, and understanding is assumed. Few organizations pause to examine the gap between knowing a feature and applying it responsibly.

Dashboards add another layer of illusion. They provide visibility without interpretation. Leaders see activity and assume control, mistaking observability for effectiveness.

At this stage, everything looks fine. Nothing obvious is broken. Metrics glow green. The narrative feels solid. And that is precisely when governance begins to erode, quietly, almost invisibly.

The real challenge isn't scaling the technology; it's scaling the judgment required to use it wisely. Without that, organizations risk building confidence on fragile foundations.

GOVERNANCE THEATER

Organizations often invest significant energy in crafting AI governance frameworks. Policies are drafted, standards articulated, procedures reviewed, and committees convened. Roles are assigned, and on paper, everything appears robust and deliberate.

Yet the essential question frequently goes unanswered: How does governance actually function in daily operations?

Most governance documents outline what should happen or what must be avoided, but they rarely explain how decisions are made in real time. There is no rhythm to guide action, no clear chain of accountability for judgment calls, and little agreement on when to intervene versus when to trust the system.

Consider common examples: persona management is formally defined, but no one actively monitors personas. Approval workflows exist, yet no one owns the consequences when those workflows stall. Human-in-the-loop safeguards are specified, but no one anticipates what happens when the designated human is overloaded.

This gap is not the result of negligence. It stems from the reality that governance is costly, uncomfortable, and hard to scale. It demands human effort beyond technology. It requires coordination across functions and leaders who remain engaged long after the ink on the policy dries. Many organizations hesitate to bear that ongoing cost.

As a result, governance often becomes symbolic, a compliance checkbox, a protective shield, a signal of responsibility without the substance to enforce it.

Failure rarely begins with broken policy. It starts earlier, when leaders stop interpreting behavior and instead delegate judgment to documents and tools. Governance collapses when it shifts from an active discipline to a passive artifact.

The real challenge is not writing the rules but sustaining the human judgment that makes those rules meaningful. Without that, governance is theater, not practice.

BEHAVIOR HAS NO INPUTS OR OUTPUTS

One reason governance often falters is that it rarely aligns neatly with the structured logic of technical processes. Most systems are designed around predictable workflows: data enters, a defined operation occurs, and a measurable output emerges. In such environments, controls can be automated with confidence.

Human behavior, however, resists this kind of determinism. Decisions are influenced by judgment, hesitation, ambition, and even identity. These factors leave traces in logs, but they do not follow a straight path from cause to effect. They bend under pressure, incentives, and context, making them far less predictable than a system's input-output chain.

Technology can record what happened, but it cannot reveal whether the action was wise, or whether a different choice would have been better. Yet organizations often assume that visibility equals governance: if an event is logged, it must be controlled; if a rule blocks something, it must be safe; if a system permits it, it must be acceptable.

This assumption breaks down in the realm of AI governance. Many decisions cannot be reduced to technical enforcement. They hinge on trust, interpretation, and the willingness of someone to pause progress and bear the cost of saying no.

As organizations scale, these challenges compound. Exceptions proliferate, variability grows, and decision-making becomes increasingly distant from its consequences. Without deliberate attention to behavioral governance, complexity does not create control, it creates opacity.

THE FIRST DRIFT NO ONE NAMES

Behavioral drift rarely announces itself. It creeps in quietly, almost unnoticed. At first, approvals start getting bundled together for convenience. Reviews become quicker, almost perfunctory. People stop reading carefully and begin clicking through as if on autopilot. Workarounds, once exceptional, turn into standard practice. On paper, everything still looks compliant, yet the spirit of governance begins to fade.

No one sets out to undermine the system. Decisions feel practical, even necessary. Pressure builds, and leadership unintentionally fuels it without taking ownership. Governance doesn't collapse in a single dramatic failure; it erodes through countless small concessions. By the time leaders sense something is off, the new behaviors are deeply ingrained. Undoing them now seems costly, disruptive, and fraught with risk. So the organization accepts the drift.

This is the point where readiness and reality part ways. The organization believes it is governed, but in truth, it is improvising. Artificial intelligence doesn't cause this shift, it simply accelerates it, turning quiet erosion into rapid transformation.

CONTROL FEELS SCALABLE. ACCOUNTABILITY DOES NOT

When organizations introduce AI, leaders often lean toward technical controls, and it's easy to see why. These mechanisms scale effortlessly. A single system can reach thousands without a single tense conversation. Guardrails are set once and rarely revisited. Dashboards provide neat summaries, audit trails appear on demand, and when something breaks, the narrative is simple: the system failed, the configuration was wrong, the vendor will fix it.

Behavioral governance is a different story. It demands human interaction, feedback, coaching, and judgment calls that rarely feel comfortable. It means confronting resistance and deciding whether someone exercised poor judgment even while following the letter of the rules. Those decisions are messy, subjective, and hard to explain with a screenshot in a board meeting.

Unlike technical controls, behavioral accountability resists automation. It cannot be fully delegated or reduced to a checklist. It requires leaders to practice what they preach, not just demonstrate compliance. And that lack of neatness makes it harder to defend when predictability is prized.

So leaders gravitate toward what looks measurable and repeatable. Technical controls offer the illusion of certainty. Behavioral accountability, by contrast, asks for discernment and courage. One feels safer, yet safety is not always where it seems.

BLAME IS EASIER TO EXTERNALIZE THAN TO OWN

When systems fail, responsibility often gets pushed outward. We point to the algorithm that behaved unpredictably, the dataset that contained errors, or the configuration that didn't align. These explanations create distance between the failure and the people involved.

But when behavior fails, there is no such buffer. Someone owns the choice. That distinction is far more significant than many leaders acknowledge.

True accountability demands that leaders step into uncertainty and make judgments that are uncomfortable. It means saying, "This action was permitted, but it was still wrong," or "The process was followed, yet the intent was ignored." These are not technical verdicts; they are human evaluations.

Many organizations sidestep this challenge by pouring resources into controls. Controls offer the illusion of rigor. They make it easier to claim compliance without wrestling with judgment. Checklists get ticked off, documents are produced, and oversight looks convincing. In reality, much of this is regulatory theater. The appearance of governance replaces its substance.

The rise of AI adds another layer of complexity. As AI systems weave into daily operations, behaviors become more visible. Patterns that once slipped through unnoticed now leave digital footprints. Decisions that used to vanish in email threads are suddenly traceable.

This visibility changes the game. For some leaders, it feels like clarity; for others, exposure. Plausible deniability erodes when systems remember everything. Connections emerge, and what was once hidden can now be displayed plainly.

That transparency often drives leaders to double down on technical safeguards. Controls feel like armor, defensible, measurable, reassuring. Yet they are not enough. They cannot replace the hard work of judgment, nor can they resolve the ambiguity that governance demands.

The real challenge is not building more controls. It is cultivating the courage to confront what those controls cannot decide: the human dimension of responsibility.

INCENTIVES SPEAK LOUDER THAN GOVERNANCE

Organizations often declare their commitment to responsible, high-quality AI practices, but the reality is shaped by what gets rewarded. Performance metrics rarely include governance. Instead, success is measured by speed, how quickly deals close, how fast code ships, how much cost is cut. In that environment, judgment becomes optional because it carries no tangible benefit.

When pausing to review AI output makes someone appear inefficient, oversight turns into a liability rather than a virtue. People quickly learn the difference between what is officially encouraged and what is practically valued. Approval gates, designed to ensure safety, start feeling like obstacles. Obstacles invite workarounds: rushed reviews, bulk pre-approvals, and click-through compliance that mimics rigor without delivering it.

On paper, governance remains intact. In practice, it becomes a performance, a ritual that signals responsibility while incentives quietly undermine it. The most corrosive factor is the imbalance of risk. Moving fast offers visible, personal rewards: recognition, promotions, praise. The consequences of mistakes, however, are delayed, dispersed, and shared across teams, vendors, and committees. Accountability becomes diluted.

Efficiency earns applause. Harm, when it surfaces, is absorbed collectively, almost invisibly. This dynamic teaches a dangerous lesson: risk-taking pays off, caution does not. Over time, unrecorded risks accumulate like sediment, layering beneath unchanged policies. The official rules still speak of prudence, but the lived reality whispers something else entirely.

AI does not create this tension; it magnifies it. By accelerating workflows and amplifying decision-making, it makes the gap between stated principles and operational behavior even wider. The question is not whether governance exists, but whether the system of incentives allows it to matter.

WHEN JUDGMENT QUIETLY ATROPHIES

When technical controls tighten, something subtle begins to happen: people stop thinking critically. Instead of asking what is right, they focus on what satisfies the rules. Compliance becomes a game of following prompts rather than exercising judgment. When the system fails to handle an unusual situation, workarounds emerge quietly in the background.

High performers feel boxed in, as if their expertise is distrusted. Newer employees lean on the system because it feels safer than making decisions themselves. Over time, the organization hardens like brittle glass, rigid, fragile, and slow to adapt. Each new control adds friction, and the pace of work grinds down. Ironically, this slowdown is often cited as justification for even more automation.

At this stage, governance flips on its head. Controls multiply, yet accountability evaporates. The structure looks secure from the outside, but resilience is quietly eroding. AI makes this vulnerability visible because it reflects reality, not policy. It learns from human behavior, not written rules. If people cut corners, AI will replicate that. If judgment fades, the system will expose it.

You cannot engineer culture out of the equation, and technology cannot substitute for human judgment. When AI becomes part of the ecosystem, the cracks in culture widen, and the cost of ignoring them grows.

RESPONSIBILITY CANNOT BE DELEGATED

One reality cannot be ignored: responsibility never transfers to machines. It remains with people. Regulators will not accept "the model decided." Courts will not accept "the algorithm chose." Customers will not accept "no one was accountable." When technology enters the process, responsibility does not vanish, it becomes concentrated.

As systems scale, the ripple effect of small errors grows enormous. Bias multiplies. Faulty assumptions spread unchecked. Invisible decisions can shape outcomes for thousands. If a human is said to be in the loop, that role must be genuine, not symbolic. Ownership must extend beyond the procedure to the result.

Risk tolerance varies. Some decisions can absorb uncertainty; others cannot. Certain applications of AI are sensible, while others should never exist. These boundaries will never emerge from code, they must be drawn and defended by people.

Executives carry more than the burden of outputs. They are accountable for the behaviors AI encourages. Does it diminish expertise? Promote shortcuts? Shift power without oversight? These questions are not obstacles to progress; they are the conditions for survival. Innovation without accountability is not advancement, it is fragility disguised as progress.

THE MOMENT RESPONSIBILITY BECOMES VISIBLE

When AI begins to operate at scale within an organization, a fundamental reality emerges: accountability becomes unavoidable. This isn't merely a matter of drafting policies or filling gaps in technology. It's a deeply human question.

Once AI-generated decisions influence customers, employees, pricing strategies, hiring practices, compliance standards, or even brand reputation, a single inquiry inevitably surfaces: Who determined this was acceptable? That question never finds its answer in an algorithm. It points directly to a person.

This is where many large-scale initiatives falter, not because the technology underperforms, but because the organization never clarified who would own the outcomes once AI moved beyond the experimental stage. During early pilots, responsibility feels shared and risk seems theoretical. Consequences appear distant, and ambiguity reigns. But scaling changes everything. Increased volume transforms minor issues into systemic challenges. Repeated patterns create measurable impact. Even silence begins to speak loudly.

AI doesn't invent this moment of reckoning; it simply accelerates its arrival. The speed and reach of automation compress timelines, forcing organizations to confront questions they once postponed. At scale, accountability is no longer optional, it becomes the cornerstone of trust and sustainability.

READINESS WAS NEVER PROCEDURAL

Organizations often believe that readiness can be achieved by producing documentation and ticking boxes: policies drafted, training delivered, controls implemented, dashboards reviewed. These steps matter, but they do not guarantee readiness.

True readiness is revealed in actions, not artifacts. It appears when leaders choose judgment over speed, even under pressure. It shows in whether decision-making is rewarded or penalized, and whether individuals feel safe to pause a process without fearing career consequences. It emerges in how exceptions are handled, are they investigated or ignored? Are edge cases treated as valuable signals or dismissed as irrelevant noise? Does oversight remain meaningful when the workload grows?

These questions are not procedural; they are cultural. When readiness is reduced to compliance, governance becomes a performance rather than a practice. But when readiness is understood as behavior, governance becomes tangible and observable.

This is why governance often erodes quietly. Policies stay on paper. Controls remain active. Yet behaviors drift away from intent, and the gap between what is written and what is lived widens. Readiness is not a checklist, it is a culture that sustains judgment under pressure.

JUDGMENT IS THE CONSTRAINT

Many organizations frame the challenge of scaling AI as a race for speed, but acceleration is rarely the real obstacle. The harder problem is judgment. Unlike systems, judgment cannot be multiplied by adding servers or deploying more code. It depends on human presence, leaders who remain engaged long after the rollout, not just those who sign off at the start.

Responsible scaling is not a matter of going fast or slow; it is about discernment. Where can automation safely take over, and where does human oversight remain essential? Which decisions can absorb risk, and which ones demand accountability? These are not questions that yield neat dashboards or simple KPIs.

This work is uncomfortable because it resists outsourcing and forces leaders to grapple with human unpredictability rather than smoothing it into abstractions. That discomfort explains why so many avoid it, and why efforts to scale often collapse before they truly begin.

GOVERNING REALITY

AI does not create new risks in isolation; it simply reveals the vulnerabilities organizations have long accepted, the way decisions are made, incentives are designed, and accountability is sidestepped. These cracks existed before any algorithm appeared.

Governance rarely collapses because a policy fails. It falters much earlier, when leaders stop interpreting human behavior and begin outsourcing judgment to systems. It erodes when conversations give way to rigid controls, and when ownership is replaced by paperwork that looks convincing but means little.

The organizations that find AI most challenging are not those without technology. They are those unwilling to govern reality as it truly operates, rather than the version documented in reports and compliance manuals.

This book is not written to oppose AI. It is written to advocate for honesty, honesty about how work actually gets done, how pressure shapes choices, how incentives influence conduct, and how responsibility cannot be handed off to machines, no matter how sophisticated they seem.

Scaling AI does not require absolute certainty. It requires courage, the courage to remain accountable when speed feels seductive, to stay engaged when delegation seems easier, and to govern human behavior rather than merely managing tools.

That commitment begins long before the first system is deployed. It is the foundation that determines whether everything that follows will endure or collapse under its own weight.

The Symbiotic Limit

CLARITY IS NOT CORRECTNESS

In nearly every organization taking AI seriously, a familiar moment tends to surface. Something unclear emerges, a decision with too little context, a disagreement without an obvious resolution, or a signal whose origin no one can trace. The atmosphere thickens. People wait. Deadlines loom.

Then someone turns to the system.

The reply arrives polished and orderly, brimming with confidence. It feels like progress. It feels like motion. For a fleeting instant, the tension lifts.

That sense of relief is genuine. Yet it is also the point where many organizations unknowingly step across a boundary they never intended to cross.

Because clarity is not the same as correctness.

AI excels at clarity. It organizes chaos, highlights patterns, compresses complexity, and delivers language that sounds definitive. It never hesitates. It never wonders if something feels incomplete or ethically fraught. It never pauses to weigh the human cost.

People do. Especially under pressure.

And that difference matters far more than most leaders anticipate.

What I've observed across industries is not ignorance about what AI can do. Leaders generally understand its mechanics. What they misread is their own reaction. They are not responding to deeper insight. They are responding to relief, the comfort of feeling that someone, or something, has absorbed part of the weight they were carrying.

Workplace uncertainty rarely stems from missing data alone. It is about vulnerability. It is about being the one who must decide without enough protection, without enough certainty, and without enough distance from the consequences. AI offers that distance instantly. Not because it grasps the situation, but because it produces something that looks complete.

And completeness feels safe.

This is how coherence gets mistaken for correctness.

Clarity gives the illusion of progress even when no real decision has been made. Correctness is heavier. It demands judgment, trade-offs, accountability, and ownership. It means someone must bear the risk of being wrong. AI does none of this. It does not comprehend confidence or danger. It does not know what it means to live with the outcome.

It simply generates.

That does not make AI irrelevant. It makes it bounded.

The trouble begins when organizations, under pressure, blur those boundaries. When the need for relief outweighs the need for rigor, clarity becomes a substitute for truth. And in that moment, the system is not solving uncertainty, it is masking it.

WHAT AI ACTUALLY SEES

Artificial intelligence does not interpret meaning the way humans do; it identifies patterns. It notices repetition, correlations, frequencies, and similarities. It recognizes what occurs often enough, across enough contexts, to form a predictable shape. That capability is powerful, sometimes more powerful than human intuition.

Yet patterns alone cannot define significance. They cannot weigh acceptable risk or determine which trade-offs are worth making. They cannot foresee which decision will erode trust, damage credibility, or drain institutional knowledge months down the line. Those insights come from experience, real, imperfect, human experience. They come from having made mistakes and learning how consequences ripple through people, not just through data points.

AI offers a single, consistent lens shaped by its training. That reliability is its advantage, but it is also its limit. It cannot step beyond the boundaries of its design.

When leaders ignore that limit, they place responsibilities on AI that it was never built to bear. The result is not just flawed decisions, it is misplaced confidence. The question is not whether AI adds value; it does. The question is whether we remember what only humans can judge: context, impact, and the human cost behind every choice.

THE TEMPTATION UNDER PRESSURE

The greatest risk of leaning too heavily on AI rarely appears in technical choices. It surfaces in decisions about people, how to handle conflict, interpret performance, or predict a future that refuses to mirror the past. These are the spaces that make leaders uneasy. They demand intuition, patience with ambiguity, and the courage to act without the comfort of clear precedent.

In those moments, AI feels irresistible. It never hesitates. It always offers an answer, and that confidence can feel like relief when a leader is exhausted or burdened by uncertainty. Turning to the system seems practical, even progressive. It feels like progress, like movement. Yet what often happens is not improved judgment, it is the quiet management of emotional weight.

Leaders do not delegate thinking because they lack concern. They do it because leadership is heavy. AI lifts that weight instantly. It gives something polished to point to, something that sounds rational, something that shifts the spotlight without truly removing responsibility. Phrases like "The system recommended this," or "The analysis indicated that," or "The model projected this trend" create a sense of stability. But beneath that calm, something essential begins to erode.

Leadership is not defined by producing answers. It is defined by owning decisions. And ownership cannot be automated. AI does not carry risk. It does not bear consequences. It does not stand in the storm when a call goes wrong. That is the leader's work, the part that cannot be outsourced, no matter how advanced the tools become.

So the question is not whether AI can assist. It can, and it will. The question is whether leaders will remember that the hardest part of their role is not finding data, but holding the weight of choice when certainty is out of reach. That is where leadership lives. And that is something no system can claim.

LANGUAGE AS A SHIELD

There is a subtler dimension to this temptation, one that rarely appears in plain sight.

In many workplaces, uncertainty is not simply about lacking answers; it often revolves around the challenge of expression. How do you speak without signaling hesitation? How do you craft a message that feels steady when your footing is not? How do you advance without revealing the gaps in your preparation?

AI steps in with language that feels polished and immediate. It offers sentences that sound certain, even when the underlying doubts remain untouched. That sense of control is reassuring. It shields us from exposure and makes the moment appear orderly.

Yet, this convenience introduces a quiet separation between leaders and those they lead. People notice sooner than organizations expect. Over time, they detect when words stop carrying the weight of thought and begin to resemble manufactured output. They sense when statements are composed but not truly claimed, when language races ahead of judgment.

The erosion of credibility does not happen loudly. It creeps in when responsibility hides behind technology. The issue is not the use of AI itself, but the absence of ownership in the message. When communication becomes a mask rather than a mirror, trust fades, slowly, but unmistakably.

THE FIRST CRACK IN SYMBIOSIS

This is often the point where collaboration between humans and AI begins to weaken, not because the technology lacks capability, but because it is asked to shoulder what it cannot: responsibility, blame, and the emotional weight of trust. AI can calculate, optimize, and predict, yet it cannot feel the sting of a decision that looks rational on paper but leaves real people hurt.

When pressure mounts, certainty feels safer than doubt. Action feels easier than reflection. But action without accountability is not leadership; it is simply acceleration. And acceleration without direction rarely builds resilience.

In moments of deep uncertainty, judgment becomes the most valuable currency. If that judgment is surrendered for the comfort of automation, the relationship shifts from partnership to avoidance. The system moves forward, but the organization does not grow wiser. It becomes faster without becoming stronger.

The cost of that choice rarely appears immediately. It surfaces later, in fragile cultures, eroded trust, and decisions that seemed defensible at the time but quietly drained capability beneath the surface. These failures are seldom attributed to AI. Instead, they are labeled as "resistance to change," "poor communication," or "execution gaps." Yet the real fracture began earlier, in the instant when clarity was mistaken for correctness.

The question worth asking is this: Are we moving toward progress, or merely away from discomfort? Because when clarity replaces judgment, the illusion of certainty can feel like safety, until the consequences arrive.

WHAT MEANING REQUIRES THAT AI CANNOT ACQUIRE

There's a quiet assumption that often shapes conversations about AI, even when no one says it outright: if a system can observe enough, connect enough, and summarize enough, then understanding will eventually follow. It sounds plausible. After all, that's how humans learn, by watching, gathering experience, and refining judgment over time. The idea that more data and more context could lead to something similar feels intuitive.

Yet what I've seen inside real organizations tells a different story. Meaning doesn't simply accumulate like pebbles in a jar. It emerges from what happens next. Humans don't just interpret information; we live with the ripple effects of those interpretations. We feel the sting of being wrong. We mend relationships when choices land badly. We remember the expression on someone's face when a decision alters their path. Those moments stay with us, whether we welcome them or not.

That layer isn't about data, it's about embodiment. AI lacks that dimension. It can process oceans of information, highlight contradictions we overlook, and reveal patterns worth attention. But it never bears the weight of aftermath. It doesn't regret. It doesn't shoulder responsibility. It doesn't recalibrate its sense of right and wrong because a choice caused harm.

And that is why meaning-making cannot be outsourced. Clarity may become easier to produce, but the moral and emotional work of interpretation remains ours. Machines can illuminate, but they cannot inhabit consequence. That is a uniquely human burden, and privilege.

WHAT LIVED EXPERIENCE ACTUALLY DOES

In most organizations, meaning is rarely spelled out; it emerges through interpretation. A policy may look clear in writing yet feel entirely different when applied. A metric can seem like a signal of priority until it collides with something people value more deeply. Even a decision that appears neutral on its own can feel punitive when layered over history, trust, or power dynamics.

Humans navigate these subtleties almost instinctively, not because we always get it right, but because experience has taught us how fragile systems become when meaning is misunderstood. We carry the memory of what happens when signals are misread.

Artificial intelligence operates differently. It does not perceive meaning; it processes patterns. It can analyze tone, infer sentiment, and summarize feedback, but it cannot discern which signal matters most in this moment, with these individuals, under these conditions. That kind of judgment comes from lived experience: from having stood inside similar situations before, from knowing which errors can be absorbed and which ones alter how people engage going forward.

This is why organizations stumble when they assume that more data equals deeper understanding. Insight can reveal what is happening, but understanding predicts what it will cost. That awareness, the ability to weigh consequences in human terms, belongs only to people.

THE ILLUSION OF NEUTRALITY

One of the most alluring misconceptions about artificial intelligence is the belief that it is inherently neutral. People often equate the absence of emotion with objectivity, assume that a lack of personal interest guarantees impartiality, and interpret consistent processing as fairness. Yet neutrality should never be confused with responsibility.

AI may not hold opinions, but it operates from a perspective, a perspective entirely shaped by its training data, the information it can access, and the way questions are posed. It mirrors historical patterns far more faithfully than it predicts future outcomes, and it prioritizes repetition over reflection. This makes it powerful as a tool, but risky when elevated to the role of judge rather than advisor.

I have seen decision-makers lean on AI to mechanize judgment in the same way they automate routine tasks. Disputes are reduced to pattern recognition. Employee evaluations become exercises in signal aggregation. Strategic planning turns into trend analysis. At first, this seems efficient, even elegant. But as the scale grows, the effect becomes corrosive.

The danger does not stem from AI acting with malice; it comes from removing human judgment from the very places where discernment matters most. When leaders outsource critical thinking to algorithms, they trade deliberation for convenience. And in doing so, they risk creating systems that are not only efficient but also brittle, systems that echo the past without questioning its flaws, and that shape the future without truly understanding its stakes.

WHEN JUDGMENT GETS OUTSOURCED

The shift toward outsourcing judgment rarely happens in a single leap; it creeps in gradually. At first, artificial intelligence is a helpful assistant, offering a menu of possibilities. Soon, it begins to rank those choices, and before long, it is used to rationalize decisions that feel uneasy. Eventually, leaders turn to it instinctively, even before forming their own perspective.

This is the point where leadership roles begin to thin out. When a leader repeatedly leans on AI for decisions about people, conflict resolution, or strategic direction, an unsettling question arises: what remains of their role? That question is uncomfortable, but it is also legitimate.

Leadership has never been about hoarding information. It exists because someone must bear responsibility others cannot, someone willing to absorb uncertainty rather than redirect it. Systems cannot do that. They do not live with consequences; they do not carry the weight of aftermath.

When AI becomes a shield instead of a lens, the foundation of leadership starts to crack. People notice when decisions feel processed through algorithms rather than owned by humans. They sense when accountability turns into something abstract, detached from real-world stakes. And once that trust erodes, no amount of data precision or analytical brilliance can rebuild it.

THE HIDDEN WORK AI CANNOT SEE

Organizations often mistake visibility for reality, assuming that what appears in dashboards or reports reflects the full picture. Yet, the essential work that keeps teams functioning rarely leaves a digital footprint. It unfolds in quiet exchanges, informal mentoring, emotional balancing, repairing strained relationships, and subtle judgment calls that avert future crises.

AI can highlight patterns in recorded activity, but it cannot detect the choices and interventions that prevent those patterns from forming in the first place. When leaders lean too heavily on algorithmic interpretations, they risk diminishing the value of this unseen labor, the glue that holds collaboration together. Over time, surveillance begins to replace genuine understanding, and metrics take the place of meaningful dialogue.

People notice the shift. They adapt, prioritizing what can be measured rather than what truly matters. The result is a slow erosion of quality, often invisible until the damage is irreversible.

This isn't a flaw in the data itself; it's a limitation of its scope. Numbers tell part of the story, but the real meaning resides in the spaces they cannot fill, the gaps where human judgment and care quietly operate.

THE BOUNDARY THAT DOES NOT MOVE

As artificial intelligence advances, its strengths will sharpen: faster synthesis of information, wider recognition of patterns, and language that feels increasingly natural. It may even mimic human tone with remarkable precision. Yet one thing will remain beyond its reach, an understanding of consequence.

AI will never grasp what it means to be wrong in front of others, nor will it feel the gravity of a choice that alters someone's career or erodes trust in leadership. It cannot absorb lessons through personal cost because it does not pay any. That absence is not a flaw waiting for a fix; it is a fundamental truth that must guide how we design and deploy these systems.

A healthy partnership between humans and AI depends on acknowledging this boundary and shaping behaviors around it, rather than chasing technical illusions. When organizations ignore that reality, they trade resilience for fragility. And fragility has a way of revealing itself when the pressure mounts.

WHERE SYMBIOSIS BREAKS UNDER PRESSURE

The collapse rarely announces itself with fanfare. It doesn't arrive the moment artificial intelligence enters the room, nor when the first workflow is automated or the first dashboard lights up with insights. It creeps in later, quietly, when the weight of urgency grows and the organization begins leaning on the system not only for clarity but for comfort. That is the point where the boundary between human judgment and AI assistance starts to blur. Under ordinary circumstances, most teams manage the balance well: AI highlights patterns, people interpret them, decisions are debated rather than surrendered, and accountability remains visible. The relationship feels like a partnership. Pressure changes that equation. Deadlines shrink, stakes climb, and attention narrows to what seems most efficient. Leaders are asked to move faster, justify harder, and absorb consequences with almost no margin for error. In that environment, AI stops feeling like a helpful voice and starts resembling a lifeline. Not because anyone intended to hand over control, but because stress makes shortcuts seem reasonable. When the cost of slowing down feels unbearable, delegation to the system becomes the path of least resistance, and that is where the real risk begins.

MOTION WITHOUT OWNERSHIP

One of the earliest indicators that an organization is slipping isn't chaos, it's motion without accountability. Things appear to hum along: AI drafts proposals, circulates updates, condenses reports, and refines ideas. Documents shuffle from one inbox to another. Charts and summaries multiply. From the outside, it looks like momentum.

Inside, a different story unfolds. Decisions stall. Judgment waits on the sidelines. Progress becomes a performance rather than a commitment. The machine moves, but no one is truly steering.

This tendency grows stronger in leadership settings where pausing feels dangerous. When eyes are on you, activity signals competence, while reflection can look like weakness. AI amplifies that temptation. It offers leaders a way to keep the gears turning without locking in a direction, an easy path to explore without deciding, to share without concluding.

Handled with intention, that flexibility can be a gift. It creates space for learning and adaptation. But when it becomes the default, it hollows out responsibility. A vacuum forms. People begin to wonder, sometimes quietly, sometimes aloud: Who is actually making the call?

When that question lingers unanswered, trust doesn't just wobble, it erodes. Motion without ownership may feel like progress, but over time, it becomes the slow unraveling of clarity and confidence.

INDUSTRIALIZING JUDGMENT

Organizations often run into trouble when they try to scale judgment the same way they scale routine tasks. It usually begins with good intentions. AI steps in to analyze performance data, uncover patterns, and spotlight anomalies. Leaders use these insights to frame sharper questions and make better decisions.

But over time, the boundary shifts. What starts as support for human reasoning begins to replace it. Conflict resolution turns into algorithmic matching. Evaluations lean on aggregated signals. Strategic choices are increasingly shaped by synthesized trends. The nuanced, interpretive work that defines leadership gets compressed into outputs that look neat and scalable.

At first, this seems harmless. When the scope is small, leaders can still intervene, add context, and override the system when necessary. Yet as scale grows, those interventions fade. The sheer volume of data, the relentless pace, and the pressure for uniformity make overrides rare. AI-generated outputs gain authority, not because they are flawless, but because they are consistent and fast. Gradually, the question shifts from "What might this system be missing?" to "Why aren't people aligning with what it shows?"

THE CONFIDENCE TRAP

Confidence often hides a fault line. AI tends to speak with unwavering poise, rarely signaling doubt unless explicitly asked. That calm tone feels like a lifeline in high-pressure moments, offering structure when chaos looms. Yet composure without accountability is not the same as insight.

When decision-makers start confusing fluency with depth, they risk granting systems more authority than they were designed to bear. Suggestions begin to masquerade as solutions. Condensed summaries start sounding like definitive judgments. Patterns are mistaken for causes. In that subtle shift, clarity begins to replace critical thought.

I have watched leaders lean on AI precisely when their own unease should have urged caution. Instead of pausing, they accelerated. The system provided language, order, and the illusion of certainty. Emotional strain lifted, and the decision advanced. The price came later.

It appeared in overlooked subtleties, in strained relationships, in results that met technical standards but eroded trust. AI didn't create those failures, but it smoothed the path toward them. By making discomfort easier to ignore, it dulled the very signals that could have prevented harm.

The question isn't whether AI is dangerous, it's whether we notice when its confidence tempts us to stop thinking.

SURVEILLANCE REPLACES UNDERSTANDING

When pressure mounts, the urge to tighten control often grows. If AI can reveal behavioral patterns, why not track them more closely? If output feels uncertain, why not measure every detail? If trust seems fragile, why not lean on data as a substitute? These questions sound reasonable, yet they often lead organizations into surveillance without naming it.

People sense when they are being observed. Even when the language is dressed up as "insight" or "optimization," the experience changes. Work begins to look like performance rather than progress. Risk-taking fades. Informal problem-solving slips into private spaces where it cannot be seen.

The dashboards still show activity, but they miss the invisible work, the quiet interventions that prevent crises, the emotional effort that keeps teams steady under strain. AI can trace clicks and messages, but it cannot capture the conversation that never needed escalation because someone handled it discreetly.

When leaders lose sight of this, they start managing what appears on the screen instead of what sustains the system. Under pressure, that gap between visibility and reality only grows wider, and the cost is often creativity, trust, and resilience.

WHEN LEADERS ABDICATE WITHOUT REALIZING IT

When leaders begin to doubt their own judgment, the shift is rarely dramatic, it creeps in quietly. The cause isn't incompetence; it's neglect. Judgment, like any skill, weakens when it's no longer exercised.

Imagine every tough call being cushioned by an AI suggestion. At first, it feels like progress: decisions come quicker, the process looks polished, and the organization hums with efficiency. But beneath that surface, something essential erodes. Leaders trade depth for speed, confidence for convenience. They become fluent in interpreting outputs, yet less fluent in trusting their own instincts.

This is leadership de-skilling, and it hides well. Metrics improve, dashboards glow, and the system seems smarter than ever, until reality shifts. Then the questions surface: When the algorithm stumbles, will the leader notice? When circumstances change, can they pivot without a prompt? When data insists on one path but experience whispers another, will they have the courage to pause and weigh both?

If the answer is no, the partnership isn't a partnership anymore. It's dependency. And by the time that becomes clear, the cost is already high.

THE REAL TEST OF SYMBIOSIS

A single question can uncover whether true symbiosis exists:

If the system vanished tomorrow, would the organization still operate with confidence? Not flawlessly, not at peak efficiency, but with enough competence to keep moving forward.

Could people still think through complex choices? Would leaders feel prepared to make decisions and own them? Could teams interpret what's happening and adapt without waiting for automated outputs?

If the honest answer is no, then what's been built isn't partnership, it's dependency. And dependency is fragile; it crumbles under stress.

Real symbiosis doesn't erase discomfort. It shifts it to where it belongs. Technology brings clarity, consistency, and scale. Humans bring meaning, judgment, and accountability.

When the pressure mounts, that balance becomes critical. The question isn't whether discomfort exists, but whether it's distributed in a way that strengthens both sides rather than leaving one powerless.

THE BOUNDARY THAT HOLDS

When collaboration between humans and AI succeeds, it rarely feels dramatic. The shift is almost imperceptible, no sudden transfer of control, no grand moment where the machine takes over. Judgment remains human, yet the way we focus and share responsibility begins to change quietly. AI brings clarity; people retain the power to choose. That principle sounds straightforward, but in reality, it is the very point where most organizations falter. The challenge lies not in replacing decisions, but in redefining how decisions are supported.

WHAT HEALTHY SYMBIOSIS ACTUALLY FEELS LIKE

In organizations where collaboration with AI thrives, the technology is not viewed as an oracle of truth but as a lens that sharpens clarity. Its role is to surface signals worth noticing, expose gaps that might escape human attention, and condense sprawling information so people spend less time hunting for answers and more time engaging in meaningful thought.

AI should not close conversations; it should ignite them. Effective leaders pause to question what might be missing, to probe beyond the data, and to listen with intent. They bring context that no algorithm can capture, insights drawn from lived experience and human nuance. And when decisions are made, they do not hide behind the system's output; they own the choice and stand accountable for it.

That stance matters far more than any technical setting. People do not look to leaders for perfect certainty; they look for presence, for someone willing to wrestle with complexity alongside them.

True partnership with AI strengthens human expertise instead of eroding it. Over time, individuals become adept at spotting patterns because they actively engage with them rather than surrendering to automated conclusions. They learn where the technology excels and where it falters. Judgment grows through interaction, not blind reliance.

This is how symbiosis matures, not by stripping away responsibility, but by demanding that humans exercise it with greater care and intention.

THE DIFFERENCE BETWEEN SUPPORT AND SUBSTITUTION

One of the strongest indicators that a system hasn't fully replaced human judgment is this: people can still perform the work without it. They may not do it quickly or at scale, but they can do it well enough to succeed. They understand the principles the system is designed to amplify. They see what the automation accelerates, and because they know the craft beneath the technology, they can recognize when something goes wrong.

When that foundational knowledge fades, the shift from augmentation to substitution has already occurred.

This matters because speed and strength are not interchangeable. An organization can become faster while quietly eroding its resilience. It can look more advanced while losing the ability to adapt when the unexpected happens.

A healthy partnership between humans and automation protects that capability. It acknowledges that efficiency comes with compromises. It accepts that some friction is not waste but growth. It uses AI to eliminate needless repetition without stripping away the thinking that repetition once reinforced.

That equilibrium is shaped by behavior, not by code. It depends on choices about how we work, not just on the tools we deploy.

THE POINT BEYOND WHICH AI CANNOT GO

There comes a stage where clarity no longer carries the weight of progress, and responsibility steps forward. This shift does not happen because technology falters, but because the nature of the task transforms.

Until that threshold, artificial intelligence is a powerful ally. It can reveal patterns hidden in complexity, condense sprawling information into something manageable, and make sense of what feels chaotic. It sharpens focus, reduces distractions, and accelerates the pace of thought.

But beyond that point, the work ceases to be computational. When choices begin to shape lives, influence trust, or define direction, clarity alone cannot bear the burden. Accountability must rest with someone tangible, someone who can be questioned, challenged, and even mistaken, yet remain present to answer.

This boundary is immovable. No advancement in models, no surge in adoption, no growing comfort with automation erases it. Responsibility is not a product of algorithms; it is a human condition, rooted in our shared systems and relationships.

AI can illuminate the path to that moment, but it cannot walk past it. The crossing belongs to people, because decisions with consequence demand more than insight, they demand ownership.

WHY RESPONSIBILITY CANNOT BE TRANSFERRED

Judgment only exists where someone can bear the weight of consequence. This is not a technical observation but a structural truth.

Artificial intelligence operates without the burden of aftermath. It does not mend broken trust or repair strained relationships. It does not shoulder blame, nor does it carry memory forward in a way that reshapes character or future choices. When a decision collapses, AI does not remain in its shadow.

Because of this, responsibility can never truly belong to a machine, no matter how advanced its capabilities become. Yet the temptation persists: to hand over judgment when it grows uncomfortable or too intricate for human hands. But once responsibility is displaced, authority becomes hollow. Decisions may still occur, but the essence of deciding, the human presence behind the choice, disappears.

Organizations feel this erosion before they can name it. Trust begins to thin. Leadership seems remote. Accountability turns into a checklist rather than a commitment.

This is not an indictment of AI. It is the inevitable result of asking it to carry something only humans are designed to hold: the moral weight of consequence.

THE LIMIT THAT DEFINES LEADERSHIP

Every organization eventually reaches a threshold. Some approach it gradually, worn down by slow shifts, while others collide with it suddenly when circumstances tighten. This point is inevitable because it is woven into the fabric of human systems.

The rise of AI capability is not in question; its progress is certain. What remains uncertain is whether leaders will choose to uphold accountability when clarity becomes easier to achieve. When responsibility is surrendered, leadership does not advance, it disappears.

AI does not lift the burden of decision-making. Instead, it exposes where that burden has always rested. The true limit is not a technological barrier but a safeguard: a line that protects meaning, judgment, and human authority in systems increasingly tempted to trade them away.

That line is not flexible. It does not bargain or bend. It exists to remind us that progress without responsibility is not evolution, it is erosion.

An Inbox Between Us

THE NON-NEGOTIABLE TRUTH

Every organization eventually confronts a reality it has long relied on not naming: work has never happened where leaders believed it did.

Decisions were never born inside systems, processes, or formal models. Those artifacts recorded intent, but they did not generate judgment. The actual work of deciding unfolded elsewhere, in exchanges between people, in timing, tone, hesitation, and silence.

That space is the inbox between us. Not a reference to email, but to the behavioral layer where instructions are interpreted, authority is tested, accountability is softened, and consequences are negotiated before they ever reach a system. This is where alignment is simulated, exceptions are normalized, and decisions are made without declaring themselves as such.

When artificial intelligence enters an organization, it enters this space first.

Not as an upgrade, and not as a replacement, but as a presence inside the conversations where work already lives. That shift alters the operating conditions immediately. What was once informal stops being ephemeral. What was once negotiable begins to accumulate.

Before AI, ambiguity functioned as protection. It allowed decisions to remain provisional, values to flex by context, and inconsistencies to pass as situational. Organizations depended on this fog. It made coordination survivable without forcing resolution.

AI changes nothing about human behavior. It changes what behavior can no longer escape.

By reading, correlating, and retaining the fragments that shape everyday work, AI removes the assumption that patterns dissolve on their own. Repetition becomes evidence. Contradiction becomes structural. The distance between what is claimed and what is practiced stops fading quietly.

This shift is already underway. Not because AI understands meaning or consequence, but because it remembers. It does not smooth discomfort or forget for convenience. It stabilizes context long enough for behavior to be seen as behavior.

There is no return to opacity.

Organizations may choose how they respond, but they cannot restore the conditions that allowed decision-making to hide inside human fog. The idea that systems produce outcomes while people merely operate them no longer holds.

The risk is not automation or error. The risk is exposure.

AI surfaces what organizations have depended on keeping unseen: how authority actually moves, how accountability is deferred, how incentives shape silence, and how people compensate for broken structures without naming them.

Exposure is not neutral. It removes deniability. It applies pressure. It forces choices that were once endlessly postponed.

AI does not introduce a new operating system. It reveals the one that has always been running. And once revealed, it cannot be unseen.

From this point forward, success or failure will not hinge on technical capability. It will hinge on whether organizations are willing to recognize themselves in the patterns that persist when observation no longer fades.

The inbox between us is no longer private. Not because it has been invaded, but because it has been acknowledged. And that acknowledgment permanently changes what responsibility requires.

BEHAVIORAL SYNTHESIS: WHAT THIS REVEALS

Across industries and organizational layers, the same behaviors surface with striking regularity. Titles change, incentives shift, vocabularies vary, but the behavior remains recognizable.

Work advances not because a process dictates it should, but because someone decides the risk is acceptable, the timing workable, or the political cost manageable. Decisions stall not because data is missing, but because clarity threatens relationships, exposure jeopardizes status, and accountability narrows options.

Email threads grow longer without sharpening their point. Meetings end with alignment language yet spawn contradictory follow-ups. Documents are revised repeatedly without altering the decision they were meant to support. Escalations are framed as requests for guidance when they are attempts to shift risk elsewhere.

These are not failures of skill or discipline. They are adaptive responses to systems that reward caution, ambiguity, and deniability more reliably than decisiveness or candor.

Organizations rarely suffer from lack of intelligence. What they lack is alignment between what is spoken, what is incentivized, and what is tolerated. People learn quickly which truths accelerate progress and which create friction. Over time, they adjust, not out of cynicism, but out of necessity.

The inbox becomes the proving ground. It is where individuals test boundaries without consequence, where they discern which leaders value clarity and which prefer comfort, where they gauge whether escalation will resolve issues or simply redistribute anxiety. It is where they decide whether naming a problem will lead to progress or punishment.

From the outside, these behaviors resemble inefficiency or resistance. From the inside, they look like careful navigation through power, incentives, and uncertainty. They look like people doing enough to keep work moving while avoiding becoming the focal point of blame.

Formal systems never replaced this informal layer. They sat atop it. Workflow tools, governance frameworks, operating models, and dashboards all assumed decisions would flow as designed. When they did not, blame fell on people for misusing, bypassing, or failing to adopt the system.

That explanation misses the essence of the problem.

People did not circumvent systems because they craved disorder. They did so because systems cannot negotiate meaning, fear, or accountability. Systems cannot sense when a decision is politically premature. They cannot interpret when a truth will land as a threat. They cannot delay action strategically to avoid igniting conflict.

So people built parallel paths. They used email to soften directives, to pre-align before meetings, to test language, to quietly veto initiatives without formally rejecting them. The more rigid the system became, the more intricate the informal layer grew.

This is why transformation efforts so often felt performative. The visible structure changed, but the lived behavior adapted around it.

Avoidance concentrates where incentives are misaligned and consequences remain unclear. Leaders often assume hesitation at lower levels signals lack of courage or competence. Ambiguity flows downward from the top.

When leaders punish bad news, uncertainty is concealed. When they reward alignment language over honest dissent, disagreement migrates offstage. When they defer decisions without naming tradeoffs, others learn to do the same.

The inbox becomes more than an operational record. It becomes an emotional one. It captures hesitation, deflection, reassurance, and quiet resistance. It reveals who feels safe naming reality and who does not. It shows which risks can be discussed openly and which must be managed indirectly.

Data has always been downstream of behavior. Long before information enters a system, it is shaped by human judgment. What gets recorded, delayed, rephrased, or omitted are all behavioral choices. The cleanliness or messiness of data is not accidental; it reflects the environment in which it was produced.

Organizations often treat data quality as a technical issue. They invest in tools, standards, and controls while leaving underlying behaviors untouched. The same incentives that shape communication shape data. People optimize for safety, not accuracy. They provide what is sufficient to proceed without increasing personal exposure.

People are not dishonest. They tell the truth they believe the system can absorb.

This leads to a sobering realization: organizations already know far more than they act on. The problem has never been lack of insight. It has been lack of consequence alignment. When knowing does not obligate deciding, information accumulates without resolution.

The inbox enables this accumulation. It allows organizations to hold contradictions without resolving them. A strategy can be endorsed in principle yet undermined in practice. A risk can be acknowledged yet indefinitely deferred. Accountability can be discussed without being assigned.

For decades, this was survivable because invisibility carried little cost. Fragmentation was normal. Memory was short. Context dissolved as people changed roles, left organizations, or simply forgot last quarter's debate.

This condition created a quiet equilibrium, not efficient, but stable. People learned how to operate within it. Leaders learned how to appear decisive without closing off optionality. Organizations learned how to function without fully confronting their own behavior.

AI disrupts this equilibrium by removing friction from observation. Patterns that once required years of proximity to detect can now be surfaced through consistency alone.

This does not mean AI knows what to do with those patterns. It means they can no longer be ignored.

The inbox was never a side channel. It was the channel. The rest of the organization arranged itself around it.

With AI embedded in that space, the behaviors traced throughout this book are no longer private adaptations. They become organizational facts.

And once behavior becomes visible, it ceases to be neutral. It demands interpretation. It creates pressure. It raises questions that can no longer be safely postponed.

That is the ground on which everything that follows must stand.

AI'S ENTRY POINT: WHY THE INBOX CHANGES EVERYTHING

AI does not enter through strategy. It enters through the inbox.

Not because email matters more than systems, but because the inbox is where organizations negotiate meaning before committing to record. Instructions are softened. Decisions delay without refusal. Power moves through tone and timing, not authority. For decades, this space survived on fragmentation. Messages scattered. Memory resided in individuals. Patterns repeated but dissolved before confrontation.

AI stabilizes memory. It retains what humans forget, correlates what isolation once protected, and places side by side what separation allowed to coexist. The inbox becomes critical because it holds behavior before formalization. Uncertainty appears as language. People explain themselves before explaining outcomes. AI does not interpret this; it simply stops erasing it.

Inconsistency has always been normal. Leaders contradict. Priorities shift. Context changes. What made this survivable was that inconsistency never confronted itself. Each thread lived isolated. Each audience heard a different story. Exceptions justified as situational.

AI places fragments side by side until their shape becomes undeniable. It does not condemn; it compares. A single cautious email means little. A pattern of caution around the same decision tells a story. One delay can be explained. Consistent delay across similar requests cannot.

This is not surveillance. It is the collapse of narrative insulation.

Before AI, organizations sustained multiple truths. Leaders believed decisions were clear because forums felt clear. Teams believed priorities were unstable because they experienced instability. Both true, never colliding. AI creates collision by connecting conversations across boundaries. The gap between intention and experience stops being theoretical.

AI does not become an authority. It becomes a witness. And witnesses change behavior even in silence.

Authority has operated through selective visibility. Risk through partial disclosure. Accountability through diffusion. AI does not dismantle these dynamics. It removes the condition that allowed them to persist unnoticed: forgetting.

The inbox was always where organizations told the truth in fragments. AI is the first participant that does not let those fragments fade. What follows is not driven by capability. It is driven by how humans respond when the stories they told themselves begin to converge.

That convergence is where deniability ends.

THE IRREVERSIBLE SHIFT: LOSS OF PLAUSIBLE DENIABILITY

For much of modern history, organizations operated without ever fully seeing themselves. This was not ignorance. It was design. Knowledge fragmented across roles, meetings, and channels. Responsibility circulated without settling. Problems were acknowledged without ownership. Decisions lingered without being formally declined.

Plausible deniability was structural, not moral. When outcomes failed, the boundary between intention and consequence blurred. Every participant pointed to reasonable explanation: context shifted, data was incomplete, guidance lacked clarity, approval was implied but never explicit. The organization moved forward, carrying ambiguity as protection.

This made scale possible. Individuals took risks without fearing permanent blame. Leaders navigated uncertainty without premature commitment. Sprawling enterprises functioned without demanding perfect alignment.

The cost was drift, duplication, erosion of trust. The pattern endured because it absorbed shocks that might otherwise have fractured the system.

Artificial intelligence closes this distance permanently. Not through enforcement, but through memory. When conversations are stored, linked, and compared across time and context, the gaps that once swallowed responsibility disappear. A concern raised in multiple forums becomes a recurring theme, not isolated confusion. A decision postponed repeatedly becomes avoidance, not prudence.

This exposure requires no intent. The revelation occurs as a natural consequence of remembering. Plausible deniability depends on forgetting, on context dissolving, on explanations fading before they can be tested against one another. AI disrupts that cycle.

Once patterns become visible, they cannot be unseen. Even restricted access or limited outputs do not restore the prior state.

The knowledge that coherence exists somewhere changes behavior. The assumption that fragmentation will shield individuals or departments no longer holds.

Inconsistency does not become failure. Organizations remain complex. Circumstances change. Tradeoffs are real. What disappears is the ability to rely on ambiguity as default defense.

Leaders believed decisions had been made when only discussions occurred. Language created illusion: "we'll revisit," "let's socialize," "pending further input" suggested momentum without closure. In fragmented environments, such phrases evaporated harmlessly. When AI detects repetition, they accumulate weight.

Values drift from formal statement to lived meaning. Exceptions occur. Tradeoffs are justified. Before AI, this drift was felt but rarely proven. With AI embedded in communication systems, the gap between stated ideals and enacted behavior becomes traceable.

This challenges a deeply rooted belief: that intention matters more than pattern. Humans explain themselves through what they meant to do. Organizations institutionalize this bias through mission statements, strategic intent, declared priorities. AI does not perceive intent. It perceives repetition.

This does not make AI wiser. It makes it indifferent to the narratives that once softened contradiction. When patterns recur, they exist regardless of how well each instance is justified in isolation. The loss of plausible deniability is not the loss of explanation. It is the loss of insulation between explanation and outcome.

Once behavior becomes legible at scale, organizations face a choice they previously avoided: acknowledge the pattern and confront its implications, or treat visibility itself as the problem.

Early responses deflect. Concerns about surveillance, bias, and misuse redirect attention from what has become visible to the tool that revealed it. The critique shifts from behavior to technology. This works temporarily. It does not restore deniability.

Even constrained AI changes how people experience their own actions. The question evolves from “Will anyone notice?” to “What story does this create over time?” That shift introduces continuity into a space that once relied on discontinuity. It prompts reflection at the moment of choice, not the moment of failure.

Accountability rarely arrives through formal enforcement. It emerges through recognition, through the moment when behavior becomes clear enough to be named. AI accelerates that moment without dictating its outcome.

The irreversible change is not that organizations become transparent. It is that they become coherent enough to confront themselves. Once coherence exists, responsibility can no longer be endlessly deferred to complexity, context, or misunderstanding. It must land somewhere.

What follows is not a technical challenge. It is a leadership challenge.

LEADERSHIP RECKONING

When the shield of plausible deniability cracks, leadership is redefined through exposure. For decades, leaders operated within systems that created distance from execution, from interpretation, from emotional weight. This was not negligence; it was the structure of scale. Email absorbed that distance, softening the edges between intent and impact. Leaders could act with good intentions and still be misunderstood. When results diverged, explanations were plentiful: complexity, miscommunication, execution failure. These stories worked until AI erased the buffer.

When behavior patterns become visible across time, leadership intent is no longer judged by what was said at the top but by what consistently happens below. This is the reckoning. It is not a verdict. It is a test of coherence. Leaders are evaluated by the gravitational pull their decisions exert on behavior. What gets escalated? What stalls? What softens before reaching them? What conversations vanish because past signals taught people that speaking up was unsafe?

Leadership influence flows through response patterns: which issues earn attention and which fade, how uncertainty is handled, whether bad news is met with curiosity or defensiveness. These signals have always existed. With AI, they accumulate into a visible record.

A leader may believe they foster openness. If messages raising uncomfortable truths consistently stall, get rerouted, or die in silence, the organization learns a different lesson. A leader may believe decisiveness is a core value. If decisions are repeatedly reopened without explanation, optionality becomes the safer strategy. Before AI, these contradictions could persist without confrontation. Each instance had its own story. Each participant could believe the problem lay elsewhere.

Now, with AI embedded in the inbox, leadership behavior acquires memory.

This does not cast leaders as villains. It reframes leadership as a system rather than isolated moments. That shift unsettles because it removes a refuge: the belief that culture is intangible and therefore difficult to measure. AI does not measure culture; it reveals consequences. It shows how leadership signals propagate, mutate, and stabilize.

Leadership has never rested on intent alone. It has always rested on the conditions created by repeated responses. AI makes those conditions harder to ignore.

Leaders now confront interpretation. Their words, silences, and reactions are no longer fleeting. They form patterns that others navigate daily. This creates pressure not to be flawless, but to be consistent enough that people can act without constantly negotiating risk.

The reckoning begins when leaders realize the inbox is no longer a private negotiation space. It has become the connective tissue through which organizational behavior is legible. Some leaders retreat: narrowing access, formalizing language to reduce exposure, pushing decisions deeper into systems to regain distance. This rarely works. Formality does not erase interpretation; it relocates it.

Other leaders embrace visibility without grasping its implications. They assume transparency will cure misalignment. It does not. Visibility without ownership redistributes anxiety. The reckoning is not a choice between opacity and openness.

It is the recognition that leadership presence now extends into spaces it once touched only indirectly.

When AI surfaces a pattern, it does not demand an immediate fix. It demands acknowledgment. Acknowledgment that hesitation has become structural. That escalation paths are being used as avoidance mechanisms. That values are being negotiated in practice in ways leaders may not endorse but have tacitly enabled. This acknowledgment cannot be delegated, automated, or resolved through governance artifacts alone.

Governance works when someone is willing to say, "This is ours." Not as blame, but as ownership. Leadership reckoning arrives when leaders understand that AI has not stripped them of control. It has stripped them of the ability to look away. Leadership is no longer about directing outcomes. It is about accepting responsibility for the behavioral environment from which those outcomes emerge.

That is not a technical adjustment. It is an existential one.

WHAT A HEALTHY HUMAN–AI RELATIONSHIP ACTUALLY LOOKS LIKE

When the initial excitement fades, a subtler question surfaces: What kind of relationship have we already entered?

AI does not comprehend culture or consequence. It does not feel the weight of being wrong. It does not bear accountability or own outcomes. What it carries is consistency. It notices repetition, detects clusters, remembers what people forget or choose not to connect. This is not wisdom. It is exposure.

In a sound relationship, humans do not surrender judgment to that exposure. They use it to confront themselves.

Most early missteps stem from asking AI to perform work it cannot do responsibly. Organizations either expect it to replace human decision-making or assume its outputs require no interpretation. Both abdicate accountability.

A healthier approach treats AI as a mirror with memory. Mirrors reveal what is present. What happens next remains human work. AI might surface that a decision is repeatedly deferred, but it cannot explain why. Humans must decide whether that delay signals caution, fear, misalignment, or something else. AI might highlight inconsistencies in applying values, but humans must wrestle with whether those inconsistencies are deliberate trade-offs or signs of erosion.

AI does not dilute responsibility. It concentrates it.

Governance cannot be treated as a technical add-on. Policies and controls function only when people actively interpret and own them. AI does not govern behavior. It makes behavior harder to ignore.

A healthy relationship accepts this without defensiveness. Leaders treat surfaced patterns as signals, not accusations. They ask what visibility reveals about incentives, fear, or unresolved tension. They interrogate the messiness of inputs rather than demanding cleaner outputs.

Trust is not built through perfection but through predictability. AI contributes by stabilizing memory, reducing the randomness of interpretation by holding context steady long enough for patterns to be discussed rather than dismissed. This works only when humans resist treating AI outputs as verdicts. The moment AI is positioned as authority, the relationship becomes brittle. People either defer to avoid responsibility or resist to protect autonomy. Both reactions distort behavior and undermine trust.

A healthy relationship keeps AI slightly off-center: present enough to notice, limited enough to require interpretation.

Patterns are not explanations. Frequency does not equal causality. Correlation does not confer accountability. Visibility is not understanding. Clarity demands judgment, and judgment demands ownership.

Humans remain responsible for deciding which patterns matter, which reflect acceptable variance, and which require intervention. AI does not resolve tension. It reveals it. That revelation removes the ability to hide behind complexity without offering easy answers in return.

This discomfort re-centers human capability. Far from diminishing leadership, AI raises the bar for it. Leaders must become interpreters, not just deciders. They must hold contradictions without dissolving them and acknowledge uncertainty without using it as an excuse.

AI does not introduce this responsibility. It strips away the distractions that allowed it to be postponed.

A healthy human–AI relationship is not about harmony or efficiency. It is about honesty under observation. AI stands in the room. It notices. It remembers. It does not intervene.

Humans decide whether to look.

That decision, repeated over time, determines whether AI becomes a tool for insight or a catalyst for deeper avoidance. The relationship itself does not dictate the outcome. Human behavior does.

AI simply makes it harder to pretend otherwise.

THE FUTURE OF THE INBOX BETWEEN US

The future of work does not arrive with a single dramatic moment. It seeps in quietly, reshaping what feels safe to say and what feels safer to leave unsaid. It changes which conversations happen in public and which slip into private channels.

The inbox remains.

What shifts is its weight.

For decades, the inbox absorbed uncertainty so systems could appear orderly. It gave people room to adapt when decisions didn't fit reality. It allowed leaders to maneuver without being crushed by consequence and employees to survive without constant exposure.

Artificial intelligence makes this space denser. Memory accumulates. Patterns linger. Explanations collide instead of passing unnoticed. The same mechanisms exist, but now they operate under observation.

This is the future the book has been circling: not a world ruled by automation, but one defined by behavioral consequence. The inbox becomes the arena where organizational truth either stabilizes or fractures.

Some organizations will retreat. They will tighten language, strip communication of nuance, and formalize exchanges until they feel sterile. Visibility becomes a liability. Work slows, becomes safer, grows brittle. The inbox overflows with compliance phrases that say little and commit less.

Others will accept that the space between people is no longer incidental. Communication is not the medium through which work flows; it is the mechanism through which accountability forms. In these organizations, the inbox becomes a deliberate space for negotiating meaning because people understand that patterns persist.

Neither path is inevitable. Both are already visible.

The future of the inbox is not about transparency as a moral stance. It is about coherence as a survival strategy. Organizations that cannot bear to see themselves clearly will blur the mirror. They will blame tools, restrict access, and confuse governance with suppression. Pressure does not disappear; it migrates. It resurfaces elsewhere. It accumulates.

Organizations that can tolerate recognition will discover that the inbox becomes less theatrical and more consequential. Fewer messages, sharper ones. Fewer deferred decisions. More explicit tradeoffs. Not because people suddenly grow courageous, but because ambiguity stops functioning as a shield.

This shift does not make work easier. It makes it more honest.

AI does not eliminate the costs of dishonesty. It exposes them.

And exposure creates a choice that did not exist in quite the same way before:

Continue treating communication as a soft layer that absorbs consequence, or accept that it is the layer where consequence forms.

This is why the inbox remains the operating system of work. It is where humans reconcile intention with reality. Where they decide how much of themselves to reveal. Where they negotiate what the organization truly is, regardless of what it claims to be.

AI enters this space as a presence that remembers, notices repetition, and refuses to forget for convenience.

There is no finish line beyond this point. No permanent equilibrium where tension disappears. Organizations drift. They adapt. They forget.

AI slows forgetting.

That alone changes the trajectory.

If AI shapes everyday work in your organization and the boundaries between people, systems, and judgment feel less clear, this book has not been a manual for what to do next. It has been an invitation to notice where you already stand.

The inbox has always whispered the truth.

Now it remembers.

And in that memory, the future of work will not be decided by machines, but by whether humans are willing to be seen by the patterns they create.

The book ends here.

The behavior does not.

Discussion Points

BEFORE YOU USE AI

These questions help you decide how and why you personally use AI tools in your everyday work.

- What specific problem am I trying to solve by using AI right now?
- Am I using AI to help me think better, or to avoid dealing with something I don't fully understand yet?
- What part of my work feels unusually difficult, slow, or frustrating right now?
- What background information do I usually assume other people already know when I explain my work?
- What assumptions am I making that I haven't clearly stated?
- If the AI gives me an answer that sounds confident, will I still double-check it?
- How will I tell whether this output is actually correct, not just well written?
- What am I still personally responsible for, even if AI helped produce this work?
- Which decisions am I comfortable letting AI influence?
- Which decisions would I feel uneasy about if others knew AI influenced them?

- If someone asked how this work was created, could I explain it clearly and honestly?
- What might happen if I start trusting AI more than my own judgment?
- What skill might I gradually stop practicing if I rely on AI too often?
- What part of my job should always require my direct involvement?
- Am I using AI to work more efficiently, or to skip over something I don't fully understand yet?

BEFORE YOU BUILD AI

These questions help a group understand whether an AI solution is being built on reality, not assumptions.

- Are we designing this based on how work is officially supposed to happen, or how it actually happens day to day?
- What human judgment are we assuming people will use to fix problems when the system doesn't work as planned?
- What information do we expect people to "figure out" that we haven't clearly defined?
- What unclear decisions are we hoping AI will quietly smooth over?
- When the process breaks down, who is expected to deal with the consequences?
- What does success actually mean for this solution, and do all stakeholders agree?
- What behaviors or workarounds must remain hidden for this system to appear successful?
- What tasks or decisions are we automating before we've fully agreed on how they should work?
- What difficult conversations are we avoiding by building this solution?
- If this system only works because people adjust their behavior without being asked, what does that say about the design?

- What extra work are people expected to do around the system that isn't officially acknowledged?
- What problems keep returning no matter how many times we redesign the process?
- Where are we prioritizing speed or efficiency over true understanding?
- If AI followed our documented process exactly as written, where would it fail?
- What truths about how work really happens would we need to admit to build this honestly?

ARE WE READY FOR AI

These questions help leadership understand what it actually means to add AI as a participant into how the organization communicates, decides, and operates.

- What new expectations are we placing on employees by introducing AI, even if we haven't said them out loud?
- What concerns or anxieties might people have when communication becomes more visible, searchable, or permanent?
- Who is likely to feel more exposed by AI, and who might feel supported by it?
- What does "using AI responsibly" mean in practice if responsibility has always been shared or informal?
- What problems are we hoping AI will fix that as a company we have never fully addressed?
- What does being "ready for AI" mean beyond technology, such as emotionally or culturally?
- What does it cost employees to quietly adapt to AI while leadership figures things out?
- What does it mean to introduce AI without first being honest about how work really happens?
- If we replaced people with AI in certain areas, what important work would no longer happen?
- What kinds of human judgment are we treating as optional simply because they are hard to measure?

- Which results depend on experience, timing, or intuition that AI would not recognize?
- What would it cost the business if we replaced judgment with consistency in the wrong areas?
- How much of our current success exists because people step in before problems become visible?

About The Author

David Dean is a technologist and practitioner with more than eighteen years of experience working inside complex organizations. His career has placed him close to the decisions, compromises, and quiet workarounds that shape how companies actually function, often in ways that formal processes fail to capture.

His work spans enterprise systems, automation, governance, and organizational change, but his focus has always been human behavior rather than technology alone. He has led initiatives meant to modernize how work gets done and has seen firsthand why many of them stall, fracture, or quietly drift away from their original intent.

David pays attention to the spaces where real work happens. Emails, documents passed back and forth, meetings where half the decisions are implied rather than stated, and the informal exchanges that determine what moves forward and what does not. These everyday interactions, more than any system or strategy, reveal how responsibility, risk, and power are actually negotiated.

In recent years, his work has examined what happens when intelligent tools enter this environment. Not as replacements for people, but as participants in a system already shaped by habit, incentive, and unspoken rules. He has observed how their presence surfaces patterns organizations have learned to ignore and forces questions that are often postponed.

This book is grounded in lived experience rather than theory or prediction. It does not argue for tools or frameworks. It offers a way of seeing how work truly unfolds and why understanding that reality matters before it becomes fixed in systems. David lives and works in the Phoenix, Arizona. This is his first book.